Che Sarà Sarà

Christine Russell
2012

The Three Birds

CHRISTINE RUSSELL

Order this book online at www.trafford.com
or email orders@trafford.com

Most Trafford titles are also available at major online book retailers.

© Copyright 2012 Christine Russell.

All rights reserved. No part of this publication may be reproduced, stored in a retrieval system, or transmitted, in any form or by any means, electronic, mechanical, photocopying, recording, or otherwise, without the written prior permission of the author.

Printed in the United States of America.

ISBN: 978-1-4669-2030-9 (sc)
ISBN: 978-1-4669-2032-3 (hc)
ISBN: 978-1-4669-2031-6 (e)

Library of Congress Control Number: 2012904841

Trafford rev. 04/21/2012

Trafford PUBLISHING www.trafford.com

North America & international
toll-free: 1 888 232 4444 (USA & Canada)
phone: 250 383 6864 ♦ fax: 812 355 4082

ACKNOWLEDGEMENTS

I would like to thank all our family and friends for their support during this very emotional time but especially our sons, Gary and Stuart, and their wives, Anna and Caroline, as they gave up their family life to be with me 24/7—also our six grandchildren, who never complained once through this ordeal.

My thanks go especially to the East Anglian Air Ambulance team and the medical staff at Addenbrookes Neurology Critical Care Unit. Without their medical care and dedication, I'm sure Derek would not be with us today. Thanks also to the local police at the scene and the Queen Elizabeth Hospital, King's Lynn, for the care given during the four days Derek was a patient there.

Please note: I have changed the names of all medical staff named in this book but have used family and friends' real names.

PREFACE

I just want you to know that the story I am about to tell turned our world upside down for months. Derek had been the most energetic person in our family. He loved being at work and was always running from A to B. He liked to get on the floor with the grandchildren and have a rough and tumble with them. I don't know who was the biggest kid amongst them. He also loved performing his Elvis concerts for charity—and then it all stopped as quickly as you could click your fingers.

I started to make notes in my diary of the day-by-day events and to record Derek's progress, so I could look back at it some time and hopefully one day read it out to Derek, but most of this story is from memory.

It was in the autumn of 2008 that I started to write this book, but every time I began to recall events, I started to cry and could not continue. There has not been a day go by when I don't think of the scene of the accident, especially when I hear the Air Ambulance fly overhead or a police car or road ambulance drive by with their sirens and blue lights on. My tummy does a somersault, and I feel sick, knowing someone is poorly, and I feel for the family concerned.

When one of the neurology guys, Bob, asked me how I was coping and I told him how I lived with the accident every day, he said that I needed to get it out of my system and suggested that I have counselling.

Then, I thought, *What if I write it all down?*

Bob said, "Yes, a good idea. Write a book."

So, here it is.

CHAPTER 1

Monday, March 19, 2007

It was early on Monday morning, when I was awakened as normal by Derek, my husband of thirty-six years, with my first cup of tea of the day. Every morning since we had been married, this was the ritual, except on the odd occasion on a weekend or perhaps when we were on holiday, when I would wake up first and make him a cup of coffee. I drink tea and sometimes would make us some toast or a bowl of cereal each and take back to bed for us to have. Well, that's breakfast in bed, isn't it?

I asked him what the time was, and he replied ten to six. He said he had not gotten to take his truck out early that morning, as it had to have an oil leak repaired. He still liked to be up early and enjoy his breakfast and watch the news. After the repairs were finished, he only had to drive about a mile along the road to load up with timber floor sections, and then he would return home and leave the next morning to deliver the load to Salisbury.

Our farmhouse is situated on the edge of the village of Wiggenhall St Mary Magdalen, our house was built around 1850. The village is situated approximately seven miles from the historic town of King's Lynn in Norfolk, England.

The population is approximately 700 residents, when I was a child the village had three grocery shops, a butchers shop, fish shop, a garage selling fuel, including a repairs workshop, a private house 200 metres further along the road with two more fuel pumps outside, the old fashioned Blacksmiths shop and three pubs (although I am told before I was born there were actually seven pubs), now sadly only one public house, the fish shop and Blacksmiths remains.

Derek had been driving a large goods vehicle for around twenty eight years, mainly delivering bales of straw to dairy farmers in Warwickshire, England. Then as dairy farmers changed to arable farming, straw haulage was not so demanding.

Gary our eldest son obtained his truck license and we purchased another truck, both trucks began hauling bags of granular fertiliser from a factory in King's Lynn to arable farmers in the Eastern region of England. Any other suitable haulage work that was in demand they would cater for.

Derek's truck could not carry as much weight as Gary's, so to make it more economical he purchased a semi trailer to tow behind his truck/trailer, both trucks could deliver their loads and get back to the yard most nights.

His mechanic arrived at the yard about half past seven, and they set about doing the repairs. Derek liked to help where he could, mostly fetching tools or perhaps driving to the industrial estate to collect a part. It was a bitterly cold March morning, so I was back and forth supplying them with mugs of tea or coffee. I glanced at the clock in the kitchen. It was half past twelve, so I made another cup of drink and took it outside to them. Derek said they had nearly finished, so I came back into the kitchen and opened a tin of vegetable soup, poured it in a bowl, and stood it in the microwave ready to heat up when he came in.

I was just listening to the one o'clock news on the radio, when Derek walked in and said he was then off. I told him about the soup, and he said he had not got time to eat, as he had told the men he would be there to load at one. I told him to sit down and eat the soup, because it was so cold outside that he needed something warm inside him. So, he sat down, and he ate his soup with some bread. As soon as he had finished it, he jumped up from the table, put on his work coat, kissed me, and said he was going and he would see me later. He thought it would take a couple of hours to load. I stood at the kitchen window and watched his truck and trailer go out of the yard, but I had this uneasy feeling that something was going to happen. I really could not settle in to do anything.

Derek was going to leave the next morning about four o'clock. He had to deliver his load to Salisbury and get it unloaded. By then he would be over the limit of hours drivers are allowed to work in one day, so he would stay on site for the night and then come back as far as the other side of Cambridge just off the M25 to load tonne hemp bales on a farm and then stay on the farm overnight and deliver the hemp bales the next morning to the hemp factory in Essex. Then, he'd return to the same farm once again and repeat the same procedure. He would take the last load of hemp Friday and not get back home until teatime. Given the price of diesel these days, you could not afford to run home empty. He did not like staying out so long, but that was part of his job.

Derek was not one for going into cafes to eat, so I always made sure he had a good supply of tinned food: stewing steak, minced beef, all-day breakfast, and tinned potatoes and vegetables. He carried a little picnic gas stove, a saucepan, and a billy can, along with the good old tin opener. Once he was loaded, he would prepare his meal by opening some tins and heating them up. He also had tinned fruit and creamed rice, and for these nights away, I always packed him up enough sandwiches, crisps, cakes, and cereal for his overnight journeys. I know—I was told that I spoiled him. I would always choose a filling that would not go bad in the heat and put as much food in a large cooler box as I could.

He had a small, portable television rigged up, so in wintertime once he had eaten, he could lie on his bed and watch telly. Some nights when I rang before I went to bed, he was a long time answering the phone, and when he did, I knew by his voice he had been asleep. He always said that at least the bed was comfortable in the cab.

In the summer months, he threw a deck chair in the cab, so he could sit outside during the warm evening, usually in one of the farm yards, and on some farms he was lucky enough to be able to use the shower and toilet block that farmers had installed for their seasonal workers.

In the cab, there were several small lockers, so when I had been shopping and bought him some tinned food and the truck stood in the yard, I would walk over to the cab and pass him the goods I had got, and he would say, "Oh, they can go in my personal cupboard."

In the passenger's side foot well, he carried a full-gallon, plastic, water bottle that he used to make hot drinks with and wash with in the morning, and there were some extra tools (just in case), water boots, and some rope. In the larger locker up on the top sat a small plastic washing bowl, along with his wash bag and towel. I told him, it was like going on a camping trip.

Anyway, that morning, I made my way upstairs to fetch the large, blue, cooler box, which was kept on top of the wardrobe in the spare bedroom. Inside was a Bakelite plate with a lid, his cutlery, salt, and a travel mug with a lid—very self-sufficient, indeed. I could pack it full, and night before he left, I would make his sandwiches and put them in the fridge, ready for him to take out the next morning. I stood the cooler box on the kitchen floor, and from the kitchen cupboard I found three plastic bowls with lids and filled them with different cereals, put the lids on, and put them in the box. I still had this uncomfortable feeling inside. I then reached for the multi-pack of crisps. I tore the packet open and went to pull some individual packets of crisps out, and something just told me he wouldn't need them. He wouldn't be going to work tomorrow, and I threw them back into the cupboard and put the lid back on the cooler box.

It was about twenty past three when the dogs outside began to bark. The one nearest to the back door was a female German

The Three Birds

shepherd called Sally. We rescued her from the RSPCA about eight years ago, and at first thought we would have to take her back, as she did not like to hear the kettle boiling or the oven or the extractor fan on. We thought she was not used to even being taken for walks, because for the first couple of weeks, she would be scared if a leaf moved or a butterfly flew by and yet she had not been ill treated. However, as soon as the back door was opened for her to go out, she would run straight to the car.

I rang the RSPCA and explained the situation and asked for their advice, and they gave me a telephone number to ring that would be able to help, which they did. After a few months, we were able to calm her down. I had to boil the kettle in the lounge, with the doors closed, so she could not hear it, and when I put the oven on, she bolted upstairs. To this very day, she still does not like the oven on, and the only time I can have the extractor fan on is if she is out of the house completely, otherwise she is petrified—yet, she does not take any notice of fireworks and thunderstorms whatsoever.

The dog that is outside all the time is a cross between a long-coated German shepherd and a Rottweiler. He just barks because Sally barks. They run to each other for support. Anyway, Sally was making a whining, yappy noise, so I knew it was not a stranger coming round. I opened the back door, and my sister Sylvia was just then getting out of the car. The dog is very much used to her, as Sylv (as all the family call her), comes round quite a bit and she fusses over Sally.

Sylv came into the kitchen, and I put the kettle on to make a hot drink. Then, we sat drinking our tea and talking, when the dogs started barking. By the tone of the bark, I knew it was a stranger coming round, so I went to the door and a man stood there. He had been round a couple of weeks previous to buy some concert tickets, as Derek is an Elvis impersonator and along with twenty other people performs on stage two concerts a year for charity and had performed a concert the week before. This man had also lived in the village several years ago and had purchased one of our trucks, and then he moved away. When he had retired from truck driving, he drove patients back and forth to the various hospitals.

He stood there shaking and said, "Mrs Russell, can you come quickly? Derek's had an accident. Do you want me to take you there?"

I said, "No, I'll take the car."

I thought if he had broken an arm, he would have to go to hospital anyway and I would be able to take him, so I ran back into the kitchen.

I said, 'Sylv, I've got to go. Derek's had an accident.'

She jumped up and went outside. Neither of us spoke to each other. I grabbed the car keys, locked the door, ran over to the garage, got the car out, and drove like hell to where I knew Derek was loading.

The truck stood on the side of the road. It is sixty feet long because it is a truck and trailer, and it was only a small yard were the floor cassettes stood ready to load. It was impossible to get in the yard at all. I stopped in front of the truck but could only see a couple standing there. As I was approaching them, I saw at the back of the trailer a lifeless body lying on the road with two men bending over it, and I noticed a small aluminium ladder lying crossways away from the side rear of the trailer toward the large conifer hedge that separated the buildings and yard from the road.

As I neared his body, I really thought Derek was dead. One man was leaning over the body, and another man was talking on his mobile phone and relaying messages to the other man, who at this point lifted Derek's eyelid and said something.

I leaned over and said. "Is he still breathing?" and his reply was, "Just".

I called out to Derek, "I'm here, Darling. It's Chris. I'm here."

And then, the man who was talking on the phone looked at me and said, "Ambulance control said not talk to him, you'll confuse him."

Then, the man with the phone relayed a message to the man leaning over the body, who he lifted up his eyelid once again and answered the other man. I stepped back and just looked on. I noticed what looked like a plank of wood under Derek. It was crossways underneath his body, and his head was lying in a pool of blood and lots of thick, clear liquid as well. Watery blood was running from his nose and ears. I thought he had smashed the back of his head open.

The couple standing there started to talk to me. I knew of them—the man had known Derek for years, but I didn't think they would have known me. They said they were looking out of their kitchen window, watching Derek over the top of the high conifer hedge, and then he was gone and they ran outside as they had guessed what had happened.

I heard one of the men say, "Where the hell are they?"

I assumed he meant the ambulance. Then, I could hear a faint siren in the distance.

Thank god, I thought, *professional help is nearly here.*

It seemed like hours before they finally drew up behind Derek's truck, but I guess it could have only been minutes. I stood back and watched, while two ambulance men took over from the other two workers from the factory. They exchanged a few words, and then the older man walked over to me. After he spoke, I realized he was the owner of the company. It was bitterly cold and the couple asked me to go inside their house with them, but there was no way I was going to leave my Derek.

Then, the owner came over to me and asked if I would like his wife to make me a cup of tea, as they only lived a few yards along the road. I told him I didn't want any cup of tea. He then took off his hi-visual jacket and gave to me to put on because I was shaking, through cold or shock, I could not say. He then handed me Derek's mobile phone and said the Air Ambulance was on its way. I needed to wear glasses for reading, which I had not got with me, so it was a struggle to see the numbers on the screen to call our sons. Gary, our oldest son was out on the road driving the other truck, and I remembered his speed-dial number was three, as I had keyed in a few speed dial numbers in for Derek one night. So, I pressed three and waited for Gary to answer. The phone just rang and rang. Apparently, he was busy loading or unloading and did not answer.

I pressed the stop button, and I remember just staring at the phone, as the lady from next door came across to me and said, "You can use our phone if you like."

I thanked her but said I was struggling to remember our other son Stuart's home number, as they had not been living at that house for that long. I just kept thinking, and then—bingo—I knew the number, so I rang it, thinking that he would be home from work by then. His phone rang and rang and rang, but no reply.

I then tried Gary's again but still no answer, and then I thought right, *I'll try Stuart again.*

After it had rung about four times, a sleepy voice said, "Hello."

I said, "Oh Stu, Dad's had an accident, and it's bad. He's fallen from the top of his load and just lays there. We're waiting for the air ambulance to come. I've tried to contact Gary, but he's not answering."

Stuart asked where we were and said he would be right there.

I looked back to where Derek was lying, but could not see what was happening because the ambulance crew were bending over him. There seemed to be police everywhere. One police officer shouted to one of the workers to go along the road and divert the traffic along a little byroad, and then he shouted to another young lad to go in the opposite direction and divert the oncoming traffic. Then, another police car turned up. I saw another policeman with a camera taking photographs.

A lady police officer came over to me and asked me some questions about Derek: name, address, date of birth, and other things I cannot now remember.

Then, all of a sudden, there seem to be a strong wind blowing and a very loud noise. I turned round and it was the East Anglian

Air Ambulance landing in the field behind us. There seem to be white debris blowing everywhere (afterwards, I learnt it was polystyrene and ash where there had been a bonfire). I ran over to where Derek laid and knelt down and opened my jacket as much as I could to prevent the dust and dirt from blowing on Derek and on the paramedics as well.

At that point, I remember asking if I could go with Derek, and the reply from one of the paramedics was, "We don't know which vehicle he's going in yet, Love."

Two men in red overalls came running over, carrying a large bag, a rucksack type bag, I think it was. At that point, I leaned against the tall conifer hedge and started to cry. The owner came over to comfort me and tried to turn me away so I could not see what was happening to Derek.

I could then hear Derek making a gurgling noise, so I pushed the owner away and went over to Derek. The paramedics were telling him to keep still. I saw he was trying to move his feet and legs, so I pressed my hands down on them hard to stop him moving. He then seem to lay quite still, so I moved back out of the way, when one of the Air Ambulance paramedics came over to me, with a pen and notepad and he started asking questions—how old was Derek and what medication was he on—just as Derek's mobile phone rang. I pressed the green button, but the paramedic shouted, "Leave it!" but I forgot to press the red button to switch it off again. Stuart was on the other end, and he heard the conversation with the paramedic. He then knew it was serious.

I told the paramedic that Derek was not on any medication whatsoever. The only time he went to the doctor's was every five years for his truck-license medical, and he never liked taking tablets. If he got a headache, which was about twice a year, he would always say, "It came on its own; it'll go on its own". With this information, the paramedic ran back to the patient and the other paramedic. I remembered at this point that, when the new surgery opened and Derek was due for his medical, I had to go with him to show him where the doctor's surgery had moved to.

It was so cold. It had just started to snow, and I looked over to where Derek was lying and all he had on was his underpants. I just wanted to run over and cuddle him to keep him warm. Then, I saw one of the paramedics cover him with a thin, silver-foil blanket, but it only just laid over the top of him and you could still see the bare left side of his body, arm, and leg.

I just stood and thought, *This is like watching a film, only this time you're in it, and he's the leading man, playing a key role.*

At this point, Gary saw on his mobile phone what he thought was his dad ringing him and returned the call. He was shocked at the news, and he said he was loading at Fakenham and would be home as soon as he could.

Seconds after that, one of the air-ambulance crew ran back to where the helicopter had landed and got in. Rotors started turning, and it began to lift into the air.

My first reaction was, *Thank god, he's not that bad, otherwise he would have been taken to hospital in the helicopter, or were they too late to save him?*

I can't say I even noticed the wind or sound as the helicopter lifted off.

I rang our friend, Keith, who lives round the corner from us and, when necessary, comes round to feed our dogs and load up the wood burner if we go away anytime, to let him know what had happened and asked him to feed the dogs. He kept a spare key to our house, in case we lost our key any time or in an emergency, but his answer phone came on, so I had to leave a message. I then rang my sister Sylv to let her know the situation because I knew she would be worried, but her husband, John, answered the telephone and said she had gone back to our house to see if I had gotten back home, so I briefly told him I was off to Queen Elizabeth Hospital with Derek and I would telephone them later.

Only seconds later, the lady police officer came over to me and said she would take me to the hospital.

The man who lived in the house next to where the accident happened said to me, "What about your car? Would you like me to take it home for you?"

I remember throwing him the keys and saying, "It's an automatic."

He replied, "Oh, I'm used to driving one of them, 'cause mine is an automatic as well."

I asked if I could go in the ambulance, and the paramedic said there wasn't room. Afterwards, I learnt that one of the air-ambulance crew was a doctor and was travelling to the hospital in the ambulance to try and stabilize Derek en route. This was why he was unable to be air lifted.

I was shown which police car to get into. The back door of the car was open so I climbed in and was about to close the door when another policeman came over to me and said I could sit in the front, as he was going in another car. So, he helped me out, and I told him I would get Derek's truck moved off the road just as soon as my son Gary got home and explained that he was on his way home from Fakenham, which is about an hours drive from our village and it would soon be dark. He told me not to worry as it was not in anyone's way where it stood. I thanked him, and I suddenly remembered I had not got any money with me. I didn't know how long I would be at the hospital, so when I saw the owner of the company standing talking to a policeman, I opened the door and asked him to lend me some money. He opened his wallet and took out a twenty-pound note. I said I only wanted some change, but he insisted I take the note.

The ambulance started to move in front of us, and to my amazement it headed toward our village. I had expected them to turn round and head for the A47, which was smoother and quicker road to travel along, and then they turned right and were going to go straight by our house. As we drove past, I saw my sister and Gary's partner, Anna, standing outside, and I wondered whether this was an omen—would it be the last time Derek would go by our house alive.

We followed the ambulance through our village, and turned left just by our house and headed toward the next village of Watlington. Then, they would drive along the main A10.

The ambulance was going very slowly, no lights flashing and no siren blasting out. At one point, it stopped for only a couple of minutes and then continued on. Once the ambulance reached the A10 and turned left, heading in the direction of the hospital, the siren went on and the lights were flashing.

The police lady said, "Sorry, Love, but I'm not allowed to put my lights or siren on or keep up with the ambulance, as I'm not actually attending an emergency now."

She was very kind and said if I wanted to use her mobile I could. I told her I had a feeling something was going to happen to Derek today. I told her I often had these premonitions, and she asked if I told peoples' fortunes. I said no, just sometimes I got these feelings and nine times out of ten they come true. I asked if she knew why Derek had fallen, and she said that the young lad who was loading the truck said the piece of wood he was standing on broke and he fell about fifteen feet to the ground. Then, I remembered the piece of wood I saw that Derek was lying on.

There seemed to be traffic everywhere approaching the roundabout on the outskirts of King's Lynn. There were three sets of traffic lights around it, and as we approached, they each in turn changed to red. It seemed as though we were never going to get there.

At last, we approached the hospital roundabout, turned left and then right, round the perimeter of the hospital, and stopped at a point where the police cars and ambulances parked.

I saw our son, Stuart, and his wife, Caroline, standing there, and they walked over to meet me. Stu said he had been coming round the Saddlebow roundabout on the outskirts of King's Lynn when he saw the air ambulance fly over him and decided to head back for the hospital, because he thought his dad was in it and they were taking him to Queen Elizabeth Hospital.

The police lady took us through the emergency doors and stopped at the A & E reception desk. Stuart and Caroline were also standing there talking to the receptionist on duty. The police lady asked us to wait in a small waiting room and someone would come and see us soon. Stuart was asking what had happened since I rang him, when a nurse came in and asked if we would like a cup of tea. Caroline and Stuart did not want one, but I did. I felt cold and numb. While we were waiting for the nurse to come back, I asked Stuart to ring the director of the hemp factory and tell them of his dad's accident as they would need to reorganise another hauler to take some hemp bales into the factory the days Derek should have been delivering there. I did not feel so cold after drinking my hot cup of tea, but I did feel a wreck. I had my old shoes, trousers, and top on, and my hair must have looked a mess, as I had been standing outside in the wind. I just could not believe that in such a short time what had happened. It just felt like a dream, or should I say a nightmare?

Just then, a doctor's voice broke into my thoughts.

He said, "Mrs Russell, your husband has a very serious head injury, and he's not responding to treatment. He needs a scan and ours is not working. Once we have him stable enough to fly in the helicopter, we will air lift him to Addenbrookes Hospital in Cambridgeshire."

I asked if he was definitely going to Addenbrookes and he replied, "Yes, we are now preparing him to go."

So, Caroline, Stuart, and I walked out of the hospital. Stuart said that he and Caroline had to give Derek's details to the receptionist and that the hospital still had our old address for Derek that we had left over twenty years ago.

We all fell silent as we walked over to where their people carrier was parked.

We climbed in and Stuart said, "We'll just go home and feed the cat and dog, take you home to sort out a couple of things, and then we can drive to Addenbrookes Hospital."

He lived just opposite the Queen Elizabeth hospital, about half a mile along the road, on a new estate. There were about twenty houses already built, and several more to be built. It only took a few minutes to get there, and once the animals had been fed, we left to go back to our house. Caroline was driving the car, and as we turned out of the road right opposite to the hospital, there on the helipad was the helicopter with its blades rotating. My stomach did a somersault. Derek was in there.

We went round the roundabout and headed along the A149 toward the Hardwick roundabout, as the helicopter flew over us.

Stuart looked up toward the helicopter and called out, "See you later, Dad. We'll soon be with you."

Stuart started to telephone around to family and friends to let them know what was happening. He also rang Gary, and they made arrangements between them to collect their dad's truck, once Gary got home.

It seemed to take forever. I just wanted to get changed and get to Addenbrookes. We arrived back at our house, and the door was open. Anna, Gary' partner as she was then, was already upstairs packing a bag for me to take to Derek. She had found some pyjamas, a dressing gown, towels, and a wash bag full of the usual things, apparently. Gary had rung her at her place of work where she was a receptionist at a hotel on the outskirts of King's Lynn. She was so upset when Gary had told her what had happened that the manager told her to go home, so she drove straight to our house, where she would wait for Gary.

When Gary arrived home in his truck, Caroline drove Stuart and Gary back to where Derek's truck stood, so Gary would then drive the truck back to the yard. Stuart stayed to help Gary rope the load up, and he drove our car home, as it was still where I had left it at the scene. When they arrived back home, they said that the scene-of-crime officers were there taking photographs. When the boys asked why, as it had been an accident and no other person involved, the police said it was just a matter of procedure and nothing more.

The Three Birds

Anna made Gary a cup of tea, and I threw some wafers and biscuits in the car along with a bottle of lemonade, as it was way past the boys' teatime and they might want something to nibble on.

We decided that we would take two cars because Gary had pointed out if one of them needed to come home, it would still leave a car at the hospital. Gary asked if he could drive our Omega since it was more comfortable to ride in than his car. We were ready to leave and Stuart and Caroline asked if I was travelling with them, but I said I preferred to sit in our car. I just wanted to ride in our car, as it belonged to both of us and I felt I would be closer to Derek. Gary and Anna were already sitting, waiting to go. Stuart waited for Gary to drive off first, as he had not got a clue where Addenbrookes hospital was, and then he followed us on the dreaded journey.

It was my choice to sit in the back of the car, so I could sit and think of all what had happened in the last few hours and wondering what we were going to find when we arrived at the hospital. Derek was an Elvis Presley impersonator, raising money for charity since 1996, and just one week previous, he had performed a show, along with twenty members of his backing team.

All Stuart had kept saying was, "I bet when we get to the hospital, Dad will be doing his Elvis stuff, strutting about in the middle of the ward trying to sell tickets for his next show."

But I knew different. Stuart had not seen his dad lying on the ground. I was dreading what we would find when we got there.

As we approached Cambridge, I started to give Gary instructions where to go—when you came to one junction, although you have to turn right, you have to keep in the left-hand lane because once you turn right, you then have to take the first left.

Gary said, "Mum, how on earth do you know that?"

I told him I could remember it as clear as anything, because about fourteen years previous, my mother was transferred from

King's Lynn hospital to Addenbrookes after she had a fall and had to go to the neurology ward for a neck and back operation. I used to drive there every day and perhaps sometimes twice a day.

Gary said, "I can't believe you can still remember it so well."

The only difference we found was once you turned right, there used to be a set of traffic lights, but now a roundabout was there instead of the lights. It used to be a very busy crossroads

I thought we were never going to get there, as once you turned left there seemed to be roundabout after roundabout and it was always a busy road. After the fifth roundabout, the tall, dark building of the hospital loomed in front of us. Although I was desperate to know what was happening, I was also very apprehensive, because I knew things were pretty grim.

Things had altered a lot since the earlier days when I had visited there. I told Gary where to park, but as we approached the barrier, a small notice read, "Staff Car Park Only", so we backed out. We rode round and round, but each car park we approached said the same thing: "Staff Only". Of course, Stuart was behind us, so it was not only us who had to reverse, but him as well. We kept taking left turns and then right turns until eventually we stumbled across the visitors' car park, approached the barrier, and pulled out a parking ticket from the machine.

Then, I really did feel sick. We were at the back of the hospital and followed other visitors, as we were not really sure where we were going, but once inside, I remembered where I was. However, because we did not know where they would have taken Derek, we discussed between ourselves and decided to go to A & E. We explained to the receptionist who we were and that Derek had arrived by air ambulance. She remembered straight away and told us to follow her. We walked through short corridors, turning left and right, until we were on the main corridor, walking up a gentle slope. There weren't many visitors along that part of the hospital.

We stopped outside some double doors, and the lady swiped her card through a machine on the wall and then pushed the doors open and held them for us to walk through. It was a long corridor with doors on either side. We were told to wait near a reception area, which basically was a desk and computer, with a closed-circuit television in the top corner behind a glass screen mounted on a wooden desk. The reception area was closed. Our lady guide disappeared through another set of doors while we stood there looking around. There were leaflets on head injuries and disabilities, but what stood out most of all were bereavement brochures.

My heart was thumping. Nurses were back and forth through those doors, and each time, I hoped they were going to come to us but they disappeared through a door, marked "Staff Only". Then, after five minutes or so, they reappeared in civilian clothes, carrying their belongings in a holdall or a small backpack, so they had obviously just finished their shift and were off home. Then, the A & E receptionist returned and said someone would be with us shortly.

From where I stood, I could see a room that had several chairs in it, and there was a telephone on the wall, a coatrack just inside the door, and a small coffee table piled up with magazines, although I could not see anyone sitting in there. I could hear voices, but the speakers must have been sitting the other end of the room.

Finally, the swing doors opened, and two men approached us. One was dressed in casual clothes, and the other one was in light-coloured blue trousers and top. The one in the casual clothes and had short, dark, curly hair and wore dark-framed glasses. He was carrying a brown folder. The other one was of Asian or Indian nationality. Obviously, he was a nurse and there to give support. The dark-curly-haired man extended his hand to shake mine and introduced himself as part of the neurology research team and the young man as the duty nurse.

Alarm bells started to ring. *Research!* My mind was racing; they only did research on *dead* people. Was I too late to say goodbye and tell him I loved him?

The two men stood quietly talking to each other, and they seemed undecided where they could take us to talk to. They eventually asked us to follow them behind the reception desk and through a door into a small sitting area with five or six chairs and a small coffee table, where they asked us to sit down.

The research guy explained that Derek had had a very serious head injury and that 50 per cent of people with this kind of injury didn't survive, but if they did, they were disabled for life. He said there were just one or two people out of a hundred who, after a few months, could walk away as though nothing had happened. Derek had also fractured the right side of his head above his right eye. The doctor went on to explain that they would have to monitor Derek's head pressure, because the brain swells and if there was not enough room in the head for this swelling, they would have to cut part of the skull away to make room for the expansion. The pressure inside the skull known as intra-cranial pressure or ICP is measured in millimetres of mercury (Hg is the symbol for mercury) must not go over twenty 20mmHg. They had to induce him into a coma to sedate him, and he was on several drugs. He had also dislocated his finger and thumb. The doctor asked if the family would let them use Derek's injuries for research, since the research they had done ten years ago was now helping him. I said I did not think Derek would have any objections to this, as he had done a lot of charity work in the past, helping other people, and this was just a different way of helping.

This research meant that Derek would have three MRI scans at different intervals, blood samples taken, and the results would be kept on database for them to refer back to but they would not keep his name with the results. He then went on to explain, until Derek came out of the coma, they would not know if he would have any disabilities. The injuries could also affect his eyesight. At some stage they might have to fit a trachea tube in his throat that could be taken out later, but then if necessary, it might have to be inserted again. Derek had cut open his right hand when he fell, and it was possible he would have to have a skin graft on it.

Stuart and Gary began asking questions about the injuries, but I just felt numb. It was really like being in a dream. Four hours ago, I was sitting in the kitchen, thinking about preparing the evening meal because Derek would not be long before coming home, and now here the family is, sitting in a small room outside the critical-care ward, not knowing what the future would bring.

Would Derek survive his accident, and if he did, would he be disabled or blind?

Then, a voice broke into my thoughts.

"Would you like to go and see him"?

It was the researcher talking.

Have you ever experienced a critical-care unit before? If not, prepare yourself as the sights you will first experience can be very daunting.

Before we walked through the double doors, we had to wash our hands with a clinical wash in a dispenser. We then followed the two men forward. There were rooms to each side of the corridor with patients lying in bed, and I expected Derek to be in one of these rooms, but we walked into an open area and round a slight right hand curve where patients were lying in bed connected to monitors and there were bleepers sounding. Finally, we came to a halt beside a bed.

An unrecognisable man lay there. The top of his head was swollen in a pyramid shape, and his eyes were so swollen that he looked as though he had had ten rounds with Mike Tyson and lost. He was on a ventilator. It seemed as though his abdomen was heaving and fighting to breathe. I suffer from asthma, and I was almost gasping and trying to breathe for him. He was wired up to many monitors, and the wires were stuck to pads on his chest. He had a needle inserted in his hand. The right side of his hair was shaven off, and a pressure bolt had been inserted, which was a white object about two inches long and about half inch in diameter. This was inserted into his skull, and at the top end of it was a wire that was linked to a monitor that recorded the pressure in his head caused by the swelling.

It was then explained to us that there would be a dedicated nurse caring for Derek 24/7, who would sit at the end of the bed, where there stood a high desk and chair. The nurses had charts to fill in every hour by studying the monitors and recording the results.

The research guy then said he would see us later and walked away.

I remember a nurse telling us that Derek had injured his right hand and probably would lose his little finger and the next one to it, as the blood was not flowing to them.

I just stood and stared at Derek. I remember stroking my hand along the side of his arm, as I dared not touch his face. He was so cold. There was watery blood draining from his nose and ears. I think we were all speechless. I know the rest of the family had not expected to see their dad in this condition, and everyone was very upset.

Derek was connected to nine monitors all around the head of the bed, and they were flashing and bleeping. I was petrified that if I moved to close to the bed I would set an alarm off.

We must have stood there about an hour, when finally a male nurse came over to us and said we should go home and get some rest and come back tomorrow. There was nothing we could do tonight, and we would need our strength for the next few days of what could lay ahead.

Although I went along, I did not want to leave. I was really sad for Derek. He was seldom ill. He had only suffered with the odd cold or tummy bug and hardly ever had a headache. The only time he went to hospital was as a visitor, mainly to visit me on the occasions I had had to stay there. He never really liked to visit anyone. He said there was a certain smell associated with hospitals that upset him, so he usually waited until the patient was well enough to go home and then he would visit them.

We followed Gary along the ward and into the corridor and came to the main doors that led out of the critical-care unit, but we could not open them. Along came a nurse, and she told us to press the green buzzer on the wall and that would open the doors to let us out.

The main corridor was empty. We walked past the rear entrance of the A & E department, and the corridor went round a left-hand bend. There were several doors on the right of us we passed, but on the left seemed to be a wall with glass or windows following the whole length of the corridor, until we came to two sets of double doors that were open on the right and led into the main area of shops, cafes and seating facilities.

We walked through this area—the shops and cafes were all closed—and we wandered around trying to find a way out. We walked the complete circle, and then Gary noticed the main entrance with its swing doors. Once outside, we then had to figure out where the cars were parked. Off we set, and finally, after some discussion, we walked the perimeter of the hospital, each in turn talking about the bright bubbly person we had had to leave behind in the hospital bed. We eventually found the cars, and after searching around for change, we paid for the parking. We had to put the white ticket that we had gotten on arrival at the hospital in the machine, and then it came up on the screen how much money to put in. It then kept the white card and produced a yellow card, which we had to put in the machine to lift the barrier up on the way out.

Before we left the car park, Gary had telephoned my sister Sylv to let her know what had happened. We could not ring too many people as it was getting late, so we decided it best to ring others the next day.

I sat in the back of the car going home, feeling as though I was a traitor for leaving Derek there on his own. I was really unaware of anything that was going on around me. We finally arrived home, and as soon as we turned into the yard, the first thing I saw was the big red and white truck standing in the shed, and there was his faithful dog, lying waiting for his master's return. Oh, boy, did my heart feel heavy.

Derek had to spend the occasional nights away from home in his truck. Due to the price of fuel today he could not afford to come home and then travel back to the same farm again, which sometimes was sixty or seventy miles away, but tonight was completely different.

Gary went to unlock the back door, while I carried the biscuits and lemonade back in the house untouched. We were soon greeted by the German shepherd, who was more a house dog. She slept in the house every night, and I felt safe with her when Derek was away. She needed a lot of fuss and seemed to know something was wrong. One of the girls made the tea, and the family decided that I was not going to be left on my own, so Gary and Anna stayed with me while Caroline and Stuart went to their home to feed their cat and dog and collect some things. They would come and sleep the night. I think they had decided on a rota system between them, as three nights during the week and alternate weekends Stuart and Caroline had their children stay with them from their previous marriages and Gary had his two boys from a previous marriage alternate weekends, but it happen to be a different weekend from Stuart and Caroline, so it was sorted who was staying which night.

Once Gary and Anna left, Stuart went outside to put some wood on the wood burner that was situated in an outside shed. He took the other dog some biscuits and generally made a fuss over him. When he came back into the kitchen, he suggested we went to bed.

I went up first and showered. As I climbed into bed and lay down, I took the empty, cold pillow from beside me and cuddled it and prayed to God that Derek would be all right.

I also asked my Mum to help me through this. During the last year of her life, she lived with us. Derek helped me to lift her in and out of the bath, and if I went out to the shops, he would take her to the toilet. During the night, she would wake up two or three times to go to the toilet. She had lost the use of her legs after she had a fall in her kitchen and hit her head on the cooker. Although she had had an operation on her back and neck at Addenbrookes, it was a fifty-fifty chance from then regarding whether she would walk again, and she never did. Although he had to be up for work at five thirty every morning, Derek would always get up when I did and help me to lift her into her wheelchair and get her to the loo.

So, please, Mum, it's your turn to help me now.

I heard Caroline and Stuart go into their bedroom and close the door. I waited a little while, and then I put on my dressing gown and slippers, crept from the bedroom, and silently went downstairs and sat in the chair in the living room, with Sally lying at my feet.

It is strange what kinds of things go through your mind in a stressful situation. I was trying to remember what Derek had said he wanted at his funeral, and I just could not think of the songs he wanted played—not hymns but Elvis songs. He said he did not want a morbid funeral. I knew he said he wanted "Space Oddessy" played as he came through the doors of the crematorium, and then during the service "The Wonder of You" and "Let It Be Me". Then, "Can't Help Falling in Love" played as the coffin was being lowered as the closing vamp. This was what he played at the end of all Elvis concerts.

This took me back to years ago, when someone suggested that we should each make a will. I remember, it was a Saturday night. My cousin and his wife usually came to see us most Saturday nights for the evening, and we thought if we had written out the wills, they could be a witness to them. I had bought a couple of bog-standard wills from a stationary shop in town a few weeks earlier, so after tea, I disappeared upstairs and left Derek downstairs to write his.

As I sat on the bed and started writing my will, Derek called out, "Where are you?"

I could hardly answer him for crying, and as he walked into the bedroom, he saw what I was doing. He said he was trying to write his will out, and the next minute we were in each other's arms crying. Coming back to reality a few years later, because we had a haulage business, we were advised to have a proper will written by solicitors, which we did. And there I sat, wondering if I would have to carry out his wishes.

All that could be heard was the clock ticking on the wall, but the hands on its face hardly seemed to move. I went to the kitchen and made a cup of tea and then went back and put the cushions up to one end of the settee and sat down, half leaning over its arm and lifting my feet up to rest them. I knew I would not sleep, but I tried to make myself comfortable. After a while, I went back and sat in the chair, watching the clock and wishing the time away.

I thought back to the day before the accident, the Sunday. It had been Mother's Day, and Derek and I had been invited to Gary and Anna's for Sunday lunch. We had a lovely meal and sat chatting until late afternoon. Then, we left to call at Caroline and Stuart's, as the four grandchildren were staying with them for the weekend. The first thing they always did as soon as we arrived was to have a tussle with Granddad, and usually the four of them would pull him off the settee onto the floor and jump on him. The three boys' favourite trick was to ruffle up his hair, as it always looked so immaculate. He always took so much pride to comb and lacquer it and to get the quiff just right at the front, and the back had to be just right. It took him three times as long to do his hair as it did mine.

How can twenty-four hours change your life so much? It crossed my mind that when he came round, he would go spare, as he hated hospitals, had had part of his precious hair shaven off, had gotten a catheter fitted, and was on medication.

Derek always said that when he went he would go as quickly as *that*, and he would click his finger and thumb together.

Had that time come?

CHAPTER 2
Tuesday, March 20

It was light enough to draw the curtains back and look outside. The birds were whistling. I sat watching a couple of blackbirds pecking about on the lawn. A dove had flown down to get a drink out of the birdbath, but doves are very nervous, and as I leaned forward to watch it take a drink, it must have seen a movement through the window because it flew off. Then, a couple of blue tits flew onto the nut feeder and were enjoying themselves until a green finch appeared and all hell broke out. The blue tits kept flying round to chase away the green finch, but he was not easily frightened. In the end, they all flew away, blue tits in hot pursuit of the green finch.

I glanced once more at the clock and it seemed the hands had hardly moved, but I knew it wouldn't be long before Caroline and Stuart would be awake, because Stuart had said before he went to bed that he wanted to get up early so he could go and feed the cat and dog and be back for when Gary and Anna arrived, ready to visit the hospital.

What would we find today?

Stuart came downstairs first, and I made him a cup of tea and he said he would ring the hospital. The previous night, when the nurse had said we could ring or visit anytime, they had given us a password to use for security reasons, because anyone could ring in and enquire after the patient. It was only the close relatives that knew the password, and then the nurse on duty could give out the information. So, about seven thirty, Stuart rang the hospital and was told that Derek had had a stable night. Although his blood pressure had dropped during the night, it had now improved.

No one wanted any breakfast, so once Caroline and Stuart had left to feed the animals, I went and showered and dressed so I was ready when they came back. My sister, Sylv, called in and our friend, Keith, and they sorted out between them who was going to feed our two dogs during the day and let Sally in the house early evening. Keith said he would take them for a walk.

All the family had arrived, and it was time to set off. This time, we all went in Stuart's seven-seater people carrier, all feeling very nervous as to what we would find when we arrived on the ward. When we were talking to the nurse last night, she explained that the air ambulance has to land on the golf course just along the road from Addenbrookes and a road ambulance then took the patient to the A & E.

As we approached the hospital, Gary said he had gone on the Addenbrookes website to find out where the nearest car park to the NCCU (Neurology Critical Care Unit) was, because the night before had been a nightmare parking. We could also purchase a parking ticket card for twenty pounds, and this would save us messing about at night-time and worrying whether we had enough change on us. So, we parked at the same car park as the night before and followed several people that were all walking in one direction, which was to the rear entrance to the hospital. Gary said we could sort out about the parking ticket later. As we walked along the corridor toward the critical-care unit, my stomach started churning and I felt sick, but we all had to be strong for each other as well as Derek.

We pressed the button that alerted the nurses that someone was waiting to enter the ward. As we found out later, there was a small television screen above the nurses' desk, and they could monitor the comings and goings of everyone. While we waited, we saw notices saying to wash your hands before you entered, and there were three or four hand-wash dispensers. We heard a clicking sound and realized we could then push the door open and walk through. We headed for the double doors at the far end of the corridor and the reception area, but there wasn't anyone at the desk, so we stood there wondering what to do when a nurse came through the doors from the critical-care unit and asked if she could help us.

We explained who we had come to see and the bed number, and she said that we could go through but we must remove our coats and hang them up on some pegs inside the waiting area near reception. The coat peg was heaving with coats. Then a couple came toward us and hung their coats in a recess area near the doors on the left. A sign said "staff only," but there were only three white coats hanging there. There was plenty of empty hooks, so we did the same. We washed our hands once more, and then we walked through the doors into the ward and walked round the bend and went to Derek's bed.

My stomach did a somersault again. His eyes were very red and swollen today. I just wanted to give him a big cuddle, but all I could do was to stand on tiptoe and lean right over to kiss his forehead.

It was a different nurse this morning, sitting on her chair at the desk. We took it in turns to ask her questions, but she could only answer questions regarding the monitors and how they functioned.

Another nurse came over and told us that there could only be two visitors at any one time, as we had to respect the other patients and visitors. She also asked if we would mind leaving for fifteen minutes or so because Derek needed to be made more comfortable. Gary and Anna decided to go for a walk to the cafeteria for a drink, and Caroline said she would sit in the waiting room. We would then take it in turns to sit with Derek.

As Stuart and I approached the bed once more, a nurse stood with her back to us and when we walked round the opposite side of the bed she was going to redress the injured hand. There was a piece of white gauze laid over it, and Stuart asked the nurse if we could look at the cut.

She looked at us amazed and said, "Do you really want to look?"

We said, "Yes."

She said, "If I show you, you're not going to faint, are you?"

Stuart said, "No, we just want to look at it."

So, she carefully removed the gauze. The gash was very deep. I can only describe it as though it was a raw, chicken drumstick that had had a large mouthful bitten out of it. You could see severed leaders and the bone. Derek looked as though he had caught it on a nail as he fell and ripped it open.

Stuart and I looked at each other, and then he said to the nurse, "But we were told he would perhaps lose his little finger and the next one to it, because the blood flow wasn't getting to it."

She took hold of his dad's hand and turned it palm side up and showed us a deep cut right across, above the centre of the palm. She then turned his hand back over and pressed each fingernail in turn too prove that the blood was flowing to all his fingers. She could see no reason for any amputation at all.

The ward doctor came over and told us that Derek had had another MRI, CAT scan, and chest X-rays. He had also fractured the right side of his head above and around the eye area. It was a good job he did not know what was happening to him.

A nurse from the bed next door walked over to help Derek's nurse to turn him over. I told her it was the first time Derek had been in hospital and she said, "Well, he's certainly done a good job of it for the first time, hasn't he?"

We were asked to leave again while the nurses got him ready for a spinal X-ray because they could not remove the spinal board he was lying on until they checked that he had not sustained any spinal injuries. We stood by the reception area outside the ward. When the double doors opened and his bed was pushed through with nurses each side and a male nurse pushing the bed and with a nurse closely following the bed with a bright-red backpack on. The pack looked like something out of a science fiction film. We later realized that the ventilator and all the wires that were monitoring Derek at his bedside were now plugged into this backpack. The nurse walking along the side of the bed assured us they would only be about fifteen minutes, so we went to get a drink. It was no time at all that they returned, and the nurse smiled and said he had no other damage, which was good news to hear.

The nurses were brilliant and really earned their money. They had to record every hour on a large sheet of graph paper the read-outs from all the monitors, including head pressure, blood pressure, sugar level, and oxygen levels. They even knew when he started to dehydrate so they could top up his fluid intake. Derek always slept with his feet out of the bottom of the bed at home, so I pulled the sheet up from the bottom, and he was wearing long, white, surgical stockings. His feet were about the only parts of him you could touch.

When Stuart saw these stockings he said, "Cor! Dad you look sexy. I'll bring in a pair of high heels for you tomorrow," hoping he would get some reaction, but he never.

The nurse then left her seat, came up to the side of the bed, and said she was going to give Derek a lung suction. She took a long tube and inserted it into the mouthpiece of the ventilator and pushed and pushed it down to his lungs to clear the fluid out. As she pulled it back out again, the phlegm drained down the tube in a small plastic tub. It was nearly black.

The nurse said, "Oh! Derek smokes then."

I told her he gave up smoking in 1985, and the nurse could not believe it.

Before then, every Saturday night when one of my cousins and his wife came to visit us, he and Derek would light up small cigars and sometimes King Edwards, which is a damned great cigar, and the living room was a blue haze. In all weathers I had to open the windows so we could breathe and be able to see each other.

Then, one night, my cousin walked in the door and said, "No more cigars, Ole Mate. I've been to the doctors, and I've been diagnosed with a heart complaint and I mustn't smoke anymore."

Derek said, "Well, if you can't smoke, then I'm not either."

And to this day, he has never had another cigar or cigarette. He often came home from work and said he had been offered one, miles away from home. No one would have known if he had accepted one, but it never bothered him.

We all felt so helpless to see him lying there with all those monitors, but all we could do was to sit and watch. You seemed to be drawn to watching these monitors, making sure each one was working or flashing, and if one made a bleeping noise we all looked scared at each other, but the nurse would walk over, remove an empty bag of used fluid, and replace it with a full one and everything seemed all right once again.

The nurse also said that Derek was going to the operating theatre in the morning to have his hand operated on, so we could not visit Derek until the afternoon.

Visitors came and went, yet nobody seemed to stay very long because nearly all the patients were in a coma, but I always felt awful to leave Derek alone miles away from home.

We had all taken turns to sit with him, and after staying many hours, in the end, we decided to leave. We had to sort out the parking ticket from the main reception desk at the front of the hospital, and then it would be an hour's journey or more getting home. Traffic was usually lighter this time of night. We needed to ring various family and friends to let them know of the situation, so we could not leave it too late to ring anyone.

We found the reception area, but no one was on duty at the desk. Then, one of the boys noticed a sign to ring the bell for attention, so he did and a security man came from a room across the other side of the reception area. Gary enquired about the parking ticket, and from behind the desk the security officer produced one and explained that we had to put it in the ticket machine at any pay station in the car park, put our money in the machine as requested, and then a two-week ticket would be produced from the machine. After that, each time we came to the hospital we could get a ticket as usual so the barrier lifted and then just feed the two-week ticket in the machine every time we left. So we followed his instructions and left for the journey home.

Gary used his mobile phone to ring a few people up to let them know the situation. It seemed to take ages to get home, but we finally turned in the yard only to see one dog looking very sad and miserable, patiently hoping that this time his master would get out of the car. The other dog had been let in the house by Keith.

We made tea and had a discussion about the previous few hours. Gary and Anna sat with me, while Caroline and Stuart went home to feed their pets. They would come back to sleep once again. I really did feel tired and worn out tonight, but whether I could sleep would be another matter.

It was no time at all before Caroline and Stuart returned, and Gary and Anna left. We decided, because tomorrow was Wednesday and it was Stuart and Caroline's turn to pick the children up from school at three o'clock, they would take me to the hospital late morning and would stay with me until about two o' clock, and then Gary and Anna would drive over to the hospital later in afternoon and stay with me until I was ready to leave at night.

Stuart went outside to see Barney and put some wood on the burner. After he came back in, I left them talking downstairs while I went upstairs and got ready for bed. I switched off the light and pulled Derek's pillow against me and asked Mum to help me once more and prayed that Derek would pull through and hoped there would be better news tomorrow. Then, I must have fallen sound asleep.

CHAPTER 3
Wednesday, March 21

I woke in the morning and remembered I could not go to the hospital until this afternoon because Derek was having an operation on his hand this morning, but I still got up early, as I once I'm awake I have to get up, unless I'm ill, of course.

So I got up and busied myself as the time seemed to be going so slow. My sister Sylv called round to see me and then went home for her breakfast as she had been called in from her early-morning job.

Stuart and Caroline got up and quickly drank a cup of tea, but before they left to go feed their pets, catch up on a few things at home get some shopping done, and pick up the children out of school in the afternoon, Stuart rang the hospital, only to be told by the nurse that Derek had had a stable night, but his heart rate was slow. She ask had Derek ever had any problems with his heart, to which Stuart told her, "No never."

Just before nine o'clock the doorbell went, and it was a friend from down the road. This friend was never an early bird, and I was amazed she was even up, let alone dressed and ready for shopping.

I said, "Cor blimey you're about today."

She said. "Well I've got an appointment in town, so I thought I would call here on the way by."

Half an later, the doorbell went again, and it was Keith's wife. She had walked round with Keith as he came to take the dogs for a walk. Sally was a bit reluctant to go with him, now that I was at home, but after some encouragement she trotted off, pulling like mad to go but pulling a lot more on the way back. Keith would walk back in the evening to feed them both and let Sally out again. He would also close the curtains and put some lights on, so he was a godsend.

I made them a cup of tea, and we sat and chatted when the first friend said she would have to go to town for her appointment, so she left. When Keith came back after taking the dogs, I made him a cup of tea. The doorbell rang again, and a voice said, "Yo ho". I knew that was the sound of my cousin's wife, Ann. After a few words were exchanged, Keith and Joan said goodbye, and they left. I said I could not believe that all the people that usually like to stay in bed where all about and out so early, but I later learnt that Gary was concerned that I would be left on my own all morning, as he had a load to deliver and Stuart and Caroline had to go home. He arranged for these different friends to stagger their visits, so I was occupied all morning. Bless him.

Just as Stuart and Caroline came through the door, the telephone rang, and I asked Caroline to answer it for me.

I heard her talking, and then she came into the room and said, "Mum," (she always calls us Mum and Dad) it's Addenbrookes. They want to speak to you."

I remember saying, "Oh, no."

She quickly told me it was nothing to worry about. It was someone from the research team wanted to talk to me. I went to the phone, shaking, and said, "Hello."

The voice the other end said, "Hello, Mrs Russell. I'm from the research unit. Do you remember saying you would give your consent for us to use Derek's medical data for research? When you come to the ward today I would like to come and meet you and explain what we do, and you can then sign the necessary consent forms."

I felt relief when I put the phone back on the receiver, because I thought they had rang to give me bad news. I remember feeling sick and had to go and sit down. I did not know whether to cry or not, and Caroline assured me everything was all right.

Ann said she would leave us so I could get ready to go to the hospital.

We arrived at the hospital about 1.00 p.m. Stuart and Caroline would only be able to stay for an hour. Again, while walking along the corridor when we are nearing the NCCU doors, my heart seemed to tighten in my chest, and I felt sick. We did the normal hand wash, went through the doors, and followed the procedure of hanging coats up and hand washing again. Caroline sat in the visitors' waiting room first, where there seemed to be several people sitting, and Stu and I walked through the doors and round the corner to where Bed 11 was. The curtains were drawn round the bed, and we stopped and stood outside the curtain wondering what was happening but after only after a few minutes, two nurses came from inside and opened up the curtains and told us that they had just turned Derek in order to make him more comfortable and we could now go to see him.

He did not look any different from the previous night when we had left him. His face was still very swollen, and his eyes were still black. We noticed a bruise had appeared down his right lower back and realized it must have been the plank of wood he had landed on.

The nurse told us that the plastic surgery team had been round and had decided not to operate on his hand until tomorrow afternoon; we had been a little concerned that it had not been operated on sooner, because of infection setting in, but I suppose they knew what they are doing.

The nurse also thought he would be taken off his sedation on Friday, which meant he would at some stage come out of his coma.

I said to Stuart, "Oh, we will have to find his dentures, as he will not like lying there with no teeth in."

Stuart just laughed and said we must try and find his St Christopher.

As soon as we sat down, we automatically seemed to be drawn to watching the monitors and to just keep telling Derek what a mess he looked. We made conversation to him, telling him about the dogs at home and stories of the grandchildren.

The male oriental nurse that was looking after Derek today was sitting finishing his paperwork at the end of the bed, so I went to ask him if he would know where Derek's dentures would be. He did not understand me at first until I pointed to my own teeth in my mouth, and he asked which hospital Derek had come from and explained they would be at that hospital.

After about fifteen to twenty minutes, I went and sat in the waiting room to give Caroline a chance to go and sit with Stuart. I sat on a seat just inside the door. It was an L-shaped room with blue chairs all around the outside of it. The outside top half of the wall consisted of mostly windows, but from where I was sitting I could not see what was on the other side of the glass. Just inside the door opposite to where I was sitting was a small kitchen area with a few cupboards and a work surface with a microwave and an electric kettle sitting on it, and there seemed to be several mugs and partly used jars of coffee. A fridge stood under one of the units and a sink along the back wall. A glass coffee table stood in the middle of the room and another one to my right in the corner, and both had several magazines on them. To my left was an old-looking coat stand, but there were so many coats hung on it, it was a wonder it did not collapse under the weight of them. Beside that was a telephone on the wall with a large message board above it where messages could be written for any of the visitors in the NCCU.

It was very hot in there because the sun was shining through the windows. I realized that there must have been a family of about five sitting at the far end. Two teenage girls kept getting up and going out and then, after a time, returning again. Two middle-aged ladies sat on the window side, talking quietly. Someone's mobile phone rang and a young girl answered it, but because the signal was poor, she left the room. On the wall at each end of the room, were two A4 notices that said in large letters "PLEASE TURN OFF YOUR MOBILE PHONE" and a picture of a mobile phone with a red line running through it. They obviously had not seen them.

I felt as though I had been in there hours, when Caroline appeared and said I should go back in, as they would soon have to leave to get the children. Just before Stuart left the bedside, Caroline crept in, and they both kissed Derek and then they were gone.

As I sat there a voice from behind me said, "Hello, Mrs Russell. We spoke on the telephone earlier. I'm from the research team."

She went on to explain that the research involved recording and keeping data on Derek, such as age, injuries, medication, blood tests, and MRI scans. Although he already had an MRI scan, he would need another one in a couple of weeks' time and then another one in six months and then perhaps in a year's time to compare the scans along with his progress. She said they did not keep the name of the patient with the data. She asked if I was still willing to sign the form and told me that at any time we could opt out of the research. I signed the form with a shaky hand. The lady thanked me, and said I could telephone the Wolfson Brain Imaging Centre at the hospital if I needed any questions answered, and she left.

I sat there a little while longer before a nurse came over and said that Derek needed turning so could I leave for about twenty minutes. She suggested I go and get myself a cup of tea.

As I made my way toward the cafeteria, there were several people coming toward me, I can only assume they were day patients going to their appointments, as I had noticed signs with several different medical departments past the NCCU doors along the long corridor. Yesterday, while we were waiting to be let on the ward, porters had wheeled patients either in beds or wheelchairs along this corridor and into the lift.

I walked round the minimarket and in the fridge saw a selection of takeaway salads in plastic bowls, so I selected a chicken salad and a chocolate muffin, paid for them, and then walked through to the sitting area. I ate my salad and the chocolate muffin, and then I went over to the hot-water machine, where there were plastic mugs with the lids in another pile and a teabag fitted to the lid, which dropped inside the mug. You just filled it up with hot water and then I thought the cup was going to be too hot to hold but then noticed a pile of folded-up cardboard holders. I opened one and stood my mug of hot drink inside it, walked to the cash till and paid for it, and then went and sat down. I gave it a good stir and when it looked strong enough drink, I removed the teabag and drank it.

I looked at my watch, I had only been gone from the ward fifteen minutes, but I guessed by time I slowly walked back, the nurses would be finished with Derek.

As I peered round the bend to where Derek's bed was I saw that the nurses had finished with him, so I sat down by his bedside once more. I had only been there a few minutes when a male nurse came over to me and asked if I was OK. He smiled and introduced himself as Nick. He seemed to be in charge of the other nurses there. He asked if I was sleeping and eating OK, which I thought was very kind of him. I told him I had just got back from the cafeteria.

He then looked at me and said, "Would you like to help me wash Derek's hair?"

I looked at him in amazement. I thought how on earth were we are going to wash his hair with him lying in a hospital bed full of tubes and wires. Nick must have realized what I was thinking, and he said he'd be back in a moment.

On his return, he put some clean towels on a stainless steel trolley, stood a large white tub down on the floor, and disappeared again. He came back with an oblong-shaped tray, which was very similar to a fibre-glass shower tray on a smaller scale, only at one end it went into a funnel shape for the water to drain down. He laid this on the bottom shelf of the trolley and set to work by lowering the head of Derek's bed, removing his pillows, and adjusting the tubes and wires, making sure they still were able to work efficiently. He moved some of the monitors on taller trolleys with wheels to one side.

He disappeared again and came back with a bin liner. He cut the bottom off and with an elastic band he fixed one end on the funnel of the tray and put the other end of the bag into the white tub, which he stood on the floor on my side of the bed.

Nick then said, "Right. Firstly, we'll have a trial run."

He lifted Derek's head up and put the tray underneath his head and neck with a rolled-up a white towel underneath his head so that the tray did not hurt his neck.

All the patients had their own wash bowl, toothbrush and paste, comb, and flannel and towels, all supplied by the NCCU. Nick then took the bowl and filled it with warm water from the small wash basin that was on the wall behind Derek's bed and stood it on the top of the trolley.

He filled a plastic jug and poured some water into the tray, only to find the water did not run straight through the bin liner into the tub—before it reached the tub, the water formed a large bubble in the liner, causing it to hang over the side of the tub so it would soon flood onto the floor. So, back to the drawing board.

He made me laugh, as he was talking all the time he was trying to come up with another idea of how to get the water into the tub. Then, he noticed another tub and stand that was used to dispose of used needles, so he removed that tub, stood his tub inside that stand, and then poured some more water in the tray, and—hey presto!—the water flowed right into the tub, because it was now higher and the bin liner went further inside.

He looked at me and said, "Do you want to wash or rinse?"

Petrified, I said, "Oh, rinse."

I thought, *I don't want to hurt his head. He must have stitches, because of all the blood that he was lying in at the scene.*

Just at this point a lady's head appeared through the curtains, and she said, "Oh, you're washing hair are you?"

She exchanged a few words with me and she was gone. Nick explained she was part of the ward team.

As Nick washed Derek's hair, you could see the watery blood running out into the tray.

Moments later, Nick laughed and said, "Oh, I see he dyes his hair, then."

So, I had to explain about the Elvis impersonator act. After Nick finished, it was my turn. Very gently I started to rinse his hair, and I asked about the stitches, but Nick assured me he did not have any and said there was not even a cut at the back of his head, which amazed me. Once Derek's hair was rinsed, Nick threw me a clean towel and said to gently dry his hair. I was very nervous as I did not want to hurt him.

Nick was clearing away everything we had used, and he looked at me and then nodded to the monitors and said, "Look at the heart rate and blood pressure dropping. He's really enjoying that." Then he said, "I'll have to get a nurse to change the sheets on the bed, as they're wet."

I looked at him and asked how they found time to wash patients' hair when they were so busy. He replied that they don't always get time but liked to if they could as it pleased so many different people: firstly, the patient feels better; secondly, the visitor is happier to see their loved one looking better; and thirdly, the staff has pleasure in knowing other people are happier. Then, a nurse came over and asked me to leave while they put clean sheets on his bed, as we had soaked them between us.

For the first time since the accident, I felt better in myself, as I had not only taken part in doing something for Derek, but also that Nick had cheered me up by involving me in his nursing care.

As I walked through the doors to the reception area, instead of walking right along to the cafeteria, I decided to sit in the visitors' day room, where today there were only a couple of people. I picked up a magazine and flicked through the pages, but I could not really get interested in reading anything.

After about twenty minutes, a young nurse popped her head into the room and said, "Mrs Russell, we've finished; you can go back in now."

Off I went to sit by Derek's beside. I had taken a reading book with me, but all I seemed to do was to watch the monitors. The nurse on duty came over and gave Derek lung suction. This began to make me feel sick, because Derek would go bright red and try to cough but no sound came out. Blood was still draining from his ears and nose.

A very well-dressed, mature, grey-haired man in a dark suit walked up to the bottom end of the bed with another doctor and four or five other younger people, who I presumed were student doctors. I looked up at them, and the man in the suit nodded his head at me. They looked at the chart and then stood and discussed it, only to walk off without a word to the next bed. I thought at least they would tell me how they thought Derek's progress was, but they said nothing.

I had taken my reading book out of my bag and opened it at the last page I had read, but it was impossible to concentrate. I found myself watching people come and go and the nurses doing their duties. The telephone seem to ring constantly. I gave up on my reading, so I closed the book and put it back in my bag.

About six o'clock, Gary and Anna came through the doors, and I filled them in on the day's events and said I would leave them to sit with Dad and I would go the cafeteria.

I sat at the table drinking my tea, and I had just eaten a chocolate muffin, when Gary and Anna walked up to the table. I instantly thought something was wrong, but Gary said they had just sat down by the bed, when Derek's two sisters, brother, and one brother-in law had come to the ward, so they left them for the little while as they said they would not stop long. Gary had kept them informed of Derek's condition on previous days and had said they could come and visit anytime.

I drank my tea and thought I would go and see them, but just as I opened the swinging doors to go through along the corridor to the ward, I met them coming out. We stood talking a few minutes. They were shocked at the state Derek was in, and soon after then they left for home.

Gary and Anna appeared, and we sat talking amongst ourselves until about five to eight and then decided to go home.

On the way home, Gary once more rang a couple of family members and friends to let them know of his dad's condition. We arrived home and the first thing as usual was to make a cup of tea, although the tea was all right at the hospital, there's nothing like a cup of tea at home. Gary and Anna were staying that night, as Stuart and Caroline had their children staying for two nights, and they would take them to school the next morning.

As the news had travelled around about Derek's accident there had been loads of cards come through the post, and I decided I would sit and open them. The sentimental words and messages inside the cards from family, friends, and neighbours made me cry. Also, there were some lovely letters from farmers where Derek had gone to load or unload over the past few years. It just went to show how concerned everyone was.

It had been another very long day. Although I was only sitting down all the time, it was surprising how tired I felt, and after seeing to the dogs I went to bed. As I laid there, I thought of everything that had happened during the day.

Caroline had said she would go to the Queen Elizabeth hospital in the morning after taking the children to school to see if they had gotten Derek's dentures and his St Christopher. I did not mind so much if we could not find the St Christopher, as I could get one from a jeweller's anytime, but false teeth would take weeks and weeks to make and he did not like being without them at any time.

I remember the night we got married, he said, "Oh, there's something you should know. I have to take my teeth out when I go to bed and put them in a glass."

I said you must be joking, and he let me believe that for a while and then laughed and said, "Not really, I only ever take them out to brush them."

What a relief that was. He had all his own teeth out when he was seventeen, as he had a gum disease. He would say to this day, that was the best thing he had done. He could eat anything with his dentures. They were never a problem to him, so that's why I needed to find them for him.

Cuddling Derek's pillow, I must have fallen asleep straight away.

CHAPTER 4
Thursday, March 22

As I woke, my mouth was really dry. I felt Derek's side of the bed and thought, *Oh, I'll soon get my cup of tea,* and then suddenly I remembered he wasn't here. I looked at the alarm clock and it was five twenty, but I still wanted to get up. I put some clothes on and crept into the bathroom to have a quick wash to wake me up and then went down stairs to make a cup of tea. While the kettle boiled, I let Sally outside, and since it was a chilly morning, I threw some wood on the burner. I think Sally and I had a race to see who could get back in the door first. I sat and drank my tea and wanted to ring the hospital to see what sort of night Derek had had, but I just could not bring myself to pick up the phone, just in case they told me some bad news.

I sat myself back at the kitchen table and looked at some of the get-well cards again. Barney started to bark, and when I looked up, it was Sylv's car pulling into the yard. She had called to see if I wanted anything and see how Derek was the night before, so she could ring my two other sisters and brother to let them know, as they knew I did not get home very early nights and left early mornings. Up to then, I just could not face talking to them. I would just collapse in tears and would not be able to talk. Sylv had a cup of tea with me and told me of all the people that had telephoned her or called round to see her. It was amazing, as some of them Derek would not have known.

The telephone rang, and my heart gave a lurch as I went to answer it. I have a caller display and I could see it was Stuart's number.

After I picked it up and said hello, he said, "It's all right, Mum. Just to let you know I rang the hospital. Dad's had a stable night, and he is definitely going for his operation this morning, so we will be at down about eleven to take you to the hospital."

After I told Sylv, she left, and soon after, I heard Gary have a shower. When he came down he told me they had heard the phone ring. We sat and chatted until Anna appeared. They had their breakfast and then waited until Stuart and Caroline arrived, as they did not want to leave me on my own.

The back door opened, and Keith shouted and said he had come to take the dogs for a walk. After a few minutes chatting, he left with Sally, who was pulling him through the gate like mad. He brought Sally back and took Barney. Once both dogs had their walk, Keith left, and I went and showered and got myself ready to wait until Stuart and Caroline arrived.

Gary and Anna left for home, because they were coming along to the hospital this evening so they could bring me home.

Once again the telephone rang, and I asked Caroline to answer it. She soon came through to the kitchen and said it was the local paper and they wanted to print a story on Derek—or, as they said, "Elvis." But as we did not know what the outcome of this accident would be, we had not told the grandchildren that their granddad was in hospital, and we certainly did not want them to read it in the newspaper—one of the grandson's classes often did a school project by looking through the local paper and choosing a story to discuss and then write about it. So, we declined the offer, and the reporter asked if we would ring them as soon as Derek was well enough and they would print a story then.

On the way to Cambridge, Stuart had to stop to fill up with petrol and also grabbed some rolls or pies to eat before they got to the hospital, as they had not had time to eat breakfast before they took the children to school. Caroline then explained she had gone to the local hospital and enquired in the A & E department about Derek's dentures and his St Christopher, but they told her that everything would have been transferred with the patient, so they should be at Addenbrookes hospital.

Some mornings there seemed to be a lot of traffic, and this morning was no exception. There seemed to be more trucks on the road, and because it was March, there were also several tractors as the farmers are busy on the land during spring time. But we got there, slowly but surely.

As we walked along the corridor of the hospital, I began to recognize different faces of people who also had a patient in the same ward as Derek. I just gave a nod or smile to the other visitors, as I felt they were in the same predicament as we were.

Caroline once again stayed in the waiting room until Stuart and I had been to see Derek. The nurse told us soon after we arrived that Derek was going to theatre around lunch time. So we all stayed for an hour, and I decided I would ride back home with Stuart and Caroline as there was no point staying because Derek would not be on the ward anyway and I could come back later with Gary and Anna.

We thought there seemed more bruising today appearing around his ears and neck. Stuart then asked why his Dad's body was so cold and yet his temperature was normal, the nurse explained that the medication they had given him kept all his organs at the right temperature inside his body, but it did not matter about his skin on the outside.

So we all left the hospital about one o'clock and made the journey home again.

It felt strange being at home during the day. I did some ironing and put some more washing in the machine, but I could not settle to do anything. I wondered around and kept looking at the clock. I just wanted to get back there to Derek.

Finally, Anna, Gary, and I were back at the hospital and walked to the bedside. He had had his operation on his hand, and it was now in plaster from above his wrist to just above the palm of his hand. It was then inserted into a blue-coloured splint, which looked very much like a ladies' Scholl sandal. It was hard based and long enough to support his wrist. Two Velcro straps went across the top of his hand. It looked as though there was a slight ridge in the base of the splint underneath his fingers, and we assumed it was to support his fingers and to keep them straight, as the surgeon would have had to repair some damage on the palm of his hand. It was resting on the top of a pillow. In my mind, I felt easier that it had been operated on.

The young nurse today looking after him told us that he did not need a skin graft. The surgeon had repaired the leaders and had filled the hole in his hand. The skin from the wound was all wrinkled up at the bottom of the thumb, so the surgeon had been able to stretch the skin back to its proper place and stitch it up.

We stayed for an hour and decided to leave, because tomorrow for us was going to be a big day. They were going to bring him out of the coma, and we wanted to be there for him.

As I lay in bed that night, I wondered what tomorrow would bring when Derek came round. Would he be able to walk, talk or even see again, as the doctors said the severe head injury he had suffered could affect his eyesight? Would he recognize his family?

We were now going into the world of the unknown, and it was now beginning to get scary.

I was scared for Derek. It would be worse for him. Yes, he was alive but, would he be disabled? This was the one thing he would never have wanted, and would he accept it, as he enjoyed life so much and loved so many things: his family, charity work, his truck driving, and his friends. He loved meeting people, and he was always a very active man.

The only thing we could do was to wait and see.

CHAPTER 5
Friday, March 23

I think everyone woke early this morning. Gary and Anna left once they had eaten breakfast, soon after nine thirty. Stuart and Caroline arrived, eager to get to the hospital. Gary was looking after his two sons from a previous marriage from tonight and over the weekend, and I insisted that he should spend time with them and keep their routine as normal as possible.

Stuart and Caroline did not have their children this weekend, so they would sleep at our house for the next five nights, as they did not have their children again until next Wednesday night.

Stuart was so excited he could not wait to get to the hospital, wondering whether his dad would be awake by the time we got there. But before we left, I felt today was the right time to ring and speak to my other two sisters. Although we are all close. I just could not face talking to them earlier. It was a very emotional conversation with both of them, but I did feel better for talking to them. I could not call my brother, as he would have been at work, so I would talk to him tomorrow morning—being Saturday he will be at home.

At the hospital, we walked toward Bed 11. Derek still laid there motionless, and we felt a little deflated. We all greeted him, but nothing. Although the bruising had started to fade, the swelling had begun moving down his lower face, and he was also now swollen all around his neck. He looked like a hamster with a stash of food hidden in pouches. After we had been there a while, a nurse came and removed two monitors that had been flashing and bleeping all week.

Stuart then asked the nurse when it would be likely that they would bring his Dad out of the coma, and she said it was a little earlier this morning. I saw the disappointment in Stuart's face. I think we all expected too much once Derek came out of the sedation. We thought he would straight away be sitting up in bed talking to us.

Doctors once again walked round each patient, took the notes from the desk at the bottom of the bed, read them, put them back, and then walked off to the next bed.

We sat there ages talking to Derek. We kept repeating to him, "Oh, come on wake up, sleepy head. We've come all this way to see you, and you can't be bothered to talk to us?"

But no response whatsoever.

The nurse came over and asked us if we would mind leaving for about twenty minutes while they turned him to stop him from getting bed sores.

As we walked along the corridor, right past A&E, I suggested that if they weren't very busy we could see if Derek's dentures where there. There were only three or four waiting in the queue at the reception desk, so we joined it. When it was our turn, we explained the situation. We were not bothered about his clothes but most concerned for his dentures. Another receptionist pointed to some white, plastic carrier bags with a black logo in the middle that were at the back of the room. She pulled on a pair of rubber gloves and started to rummage inside one of the bags. She began to pull out a child's soft toy and then a small piece of clothing. I remembered saying to her they are not going to be in there. The contents obviously belonged to a small child.

The other receptionist said they must have been thrown away. I said surely not. What if he had had his wallet in his trousers' pocket? Surely, someone checks them out. The other lady insisted that unless they had contacted relatives for permission, they were not allowed to destroy anything.

The first lady we had spoken to decided to telephone ambulance headquarters to see if they had been left in the ambulance, but they said everything would have gone with the patient. Then, they tried air-ambulance headquarters, and they said the same. After a long discussion, I asked if she would mind telephoning our local hospital because she would know the right person to talk to just in case someone had put them in a safe place until they were claimed. She asked if we would be going back on the NCCU, and said they would telephone through and leave a message if they found anything out.

We walked away, and I remembered thinking, *Derek will be devastated if he has to go weeks or even months without his dentures.*

By the time we got back to the ward, Derek had been turned and made more comfortable. We kept talking to him, hoping he would recognize one of our voices and open his eyes, when Caroline said, "Look!" Behind Derek's bed under the wash basin on the floor stood a white plastic bag. Stuart quickly went round the end of the bed and picked up the bag and passed it to me. As I began opening it, the smell from inside was like a rodent had crawled in it and died. I peered inside and could see part of a silver chain amongst some clothes. I picked out the chain, and it was the St Christopher. It was tarnished but unbroken. We had wondered whether the paramedics would have had to break the chain in order to remove it quickly when trying to administer drugs. Then, I saw something wrapped in a paper towel, and when I felt it, it was his dentures. So, I put them both objects in my handbag to make sure we did not lose them again.

We had smelt this awful smell before, but just thought it was coming from Derek's wound on his hand. We could not stand the smell coming from inside the bag any longer and asked the nurse if he had another plastic bag we could put this one inside.

We put our bag inside one and then the whole lot in the other one to try and stop the stench.

The nurse had also mentioned that Derek could have his pressure monitor out tomorrow.

We arrived home, feeling pleased that at least something good had come from the day. As we unlocked the door, Stuart asked for the workshop key, because he was going to check in the bag of clothes to make sure that there was nothing else inside them. I told him that his dad's wallet was already inside the house and I had been given his mobile phone at the scene, so there should not be anything else in the pockets—only perhaps nuts, bolts, or screws, because every time I washed his clothes I always felt in the pockets and you could guarantee there would be one or the other in them.

As I entered the kitchen there a lovely display of flowers that the Elvis team had sent to me with all their good wishes, and also their thoughts were with Derek. Of course, I stood and had a little cry again.

Caroline made the tea, and we sat drinking it. After about ten minutes, the door opened and Stuart walked in with a broad grin on his face. He always makes light jokes about everything. We have been told he takes after his Granddad Russell, who was always a joker when he was younger.

Stuart then went on to explain, because of the smell, he had to shove a piece of blue paper towelling up each nostril. He put a pair of rubber gloves on and emptied the contents of the bag on the bench. There was the top half of Derek's shirt with one sleeve attached and trousers with one leg missing. The brown-leather belt was still done up but had been cut in two at the back. Only the top right-hand side of his boiler suit and the left leg were there and a pair of socks. Stuart threw them all on the burner. By this time, Stuart had us in stitches. It was the first time we had had a giggle since the accident, and it relieved some of the tension, I can tell you. All week, my heart had felt like a lead weight inside my chest waiting to burst out. Although the boys kept telling me all week that Dad will be fine and you know him, we did not know what was going to happen, and I knew they were telling me this to ease my mind but they were just as concerned as I was.

I had cleaned the St Christopher with a special duster used to clean silver, and then I hung the chain around my neck and I said I would wear it until the day Derek was ready to put it back around his neck.

As Stuart and I sat talking in the dining room about what we hoped to find tomorrow Stuart said, "I just hope he will be able to move his limbs OK and that in time he will be his old self."

I replied, "Stuart, if he needs washing, dressing, and feeding, then I will be here to do it."

He exploded like a bottle of fizzy pop that had been shaken up.

"Mum! However can you think like that?"

I then replied, "Stuart, I've had a lot more than that to worry about this week."

He began to calm down, and after a little while I began to feel sleepy and decided to go to bed, as it would be another long day tomorrow.

CHAPTER 6
Saturday, March 24

Another new day had dawned. I was up and dressed when Sylv called round. She was expecting me to say Derek was sitting up talking. I told her I could not wait to go to the hospital to see if there was any change. I felt awful having to rely on the boys taking me backwards and forwards to the hospital. I told them I was quite capable of driving myself, but they said with all the stress of the day and late at night with all the oncoming car lights my concentration would be limited, so I was not to drive. Before we left for the hospital, I rang my brother and chatted for about ten minutes, then left for the journey ahead.

We turned the bend of the ward, hoping and praying Derek would be looking out for us to arrive, but there he lay, still asleep, almost as we had left him last night, although he would have been turned several times during the night. Disappointment spread across our faces. We all walked up to the bed and each in turn talked to him, but still no response.

He had to have the suction tube a lot that day. When the nurses pushed the suction tube down into Derek's lungs, we had to look away from the bed until the nurse had finished, because once the tube reached his lungs, Derek would cough and it was a silent cough, which made things worse. It made his face, neck, and chest go nearly a deep red. The brain pressure monitor number would go up in the fifties, and at once I would think, *Oh, my god, it must not go over twenty*, and then, just as quickly, it would drop back to normal again.

I felt as though I could have pushed the nurse away, but I knew it was their job. There was one nurse that did this suction, and Derek never moved—he would just lay there as though nothing was happening. I knew it was clearing his lungs and helping him. I also noticed for the first time that the draining had almost stopped from his ears and nose.

We sat for a while, and then all went to the cafeteria for a drink and something to eat. On our return to the ward, the nurse came to the foot of the bed and in her hand she had a pair of what looked like plaster of Paris boots. I asked what she was going to do with them. She said because Derek was laying so still, his feet had begun to droop and these boots were to support his feet in the upright position. He was to have them on for two hours and then off for two hours. The boots were open from the toes right up the front so they could easily be slipped on the foot and leg with Velcro fastenings at different intervals. The nurse finished writing her notes and slipped the boots on.

As we were talking, Stuart said, "I'm sure Dad's left hand just moved very, very slightly."

Then, both feet moved just a fraction and then nothing. We sat and stared at his feet and legs hoping we had not imagined it. His right hand was very swollen, but I thought the bruises had started to fade around the eyes, although they were still swollen.

Derek's younger sister and her husband came to see him in the afternoon for a short while. So to give them some time with Derek, the rest of us went for a cup of tea. Then, twenty minutes later, they joined us for a chat, after which we went back to the ward and they left for home.

We sat the remainder of the time talking to Derek and telling him all sorts of things to try and get him to wake but no such luck. The nurse asked if we would mind waiting just outside the curtain because they would only be a few minutes while they made Derek comfortable. As we stood there, the guy from the research team, who we had met on the night of the accident, walked over and spoke to us. Stuart asked if it was possible to see his dad's scan. The researcher said it would be no problem, and he asked us to follow him over to the desk where a computer stood. He scrolled through different data and then came to a picture, which he was able to make larger, and explained how the brain and skull area were damaged. Stuart said it looked like a walnut in a bucket, but he also asked several serious questions.

When it was time to leave, I told Derek that we would be back tomorrow and wanted to see him sitting up in bed. Of course, the conversation all the way home was about the slight movement we thought we had seen earlier.

The words I wrote in my dairy for that day were: "My heart feels as though someone is trying to pull it out of my chest. To see you lying there unable to help you, I pray for you every night to make a full recovery and come home very soon."

I looked up at the clock and realized we must not forget to alter the clocks tonight as British summer time began.

CHAPTER 7
Sunday, March 25

First thing this morning, Stuart rang the hospital excited that his dad might be conscious, but the nurse in charge just said he had had a comfortable night, so we were eager once again to get to the hospital.

I can't really remember what day it happened, but my niece, Sue, had gone to visit her friend in the town where she lived, and Sue told her the story of Derek's accident. Then, her friend disappeared upstairs, and when she returned, she gave Sue a small package to take to Derek. Sue said that her friend said I must follow the instructions on the paper. When I opened the small plastic bag and pulled out its contents, there was a green bootlace necklace made of cloth with a small, green and white oblong shape attached, which was meant to be worn at the front with a picture of Mary on it and on the reverse side was a heart with a sword through it and the words read:

"IMMACULATE HEART OF MARY, PRAY FOR
US NOW AND AT THE HOUR OF DEATH."

The paper enclosed with this necklace called it The Green Scapular.

The person who is ill should repeat the saying ("Immaculate Heart . . .") as many times as they can during the day, but I was going to have to say it on behalf of Derek. There was also a leaflet telling various stories of healing that had happened to others.

Gary had rang to see how his dad was, and said he would be along to see him later that evening but because he never usually took his two boys home until seven, I told him to leave it until tomorrow night to make the visit. He would have more time and could stay longer rather than to rush to the hospital tonight, so he agreed to do that.

Sylv had called in and as usual stopped for a half an hour's chat, and then she left so I could get ready for when Stuart and Caroline returned after they had gone home to feed the pets and catch up on a few jobs.

The dogs started to bark, and when I looked out of the window I saw another sister and her husband getting out of their car, so I opened the door to let them in. After a few tears, we sat talking. Then, my only brother, Mick, and his wife, Shirley, arrived. I made them all some tea, and we discussed all the possibilities of Derek's condition and future, although at times I could not speak for crying. I was very lucky to have all my family and friends around me, but I must admit I still felt very lonely. They were all confident that Derek would recover, since he was a strong-willed person and if anyone would get over such a terrible injury it would be him. He was always fit and healthy, and that would go a long way to help his recovery.

I just prayed they were right.

As soon as we arrived at the bedside, I took out the cloth necklace and put it in the bedside cabinet drawer, as there was no way I could put it round Derek's neck, and repeated the words several times during the course of the day.

He was still not conscious, so we asked the nurse if he had made any progress since the night before, but she had not come on duty until eight this morning. She said he had remained asleep. Then, he started to yawn and we all tried to talk to him at once, but there was no response. He seemed to be yawning more today.

As the day went on, he seemed to be moving his arms and legs more, but we could not get anything other than that. We hoped he would open his eyes or to even try to speak, but nothing.

While we went for a drink, the nurse had put a tube up his nose and down his throat into his stomach because they were going to try and feed him through this tube. So, that was another good sign.

We were more excited today, each talking and asking Derek questions. We stroked his arm, and when he had not got his boots on one of us—well, Caroline or me—rubbed his feet, which were very swollen because he had been lying still for several days. Stuart said no way; he wasn't going to rub his dad's feet.

The nurse on duty was a lovely dark-skinned lady, and she kept shouting, "Russell, Russell! Wake up, because all your family are here!"

We told her that she was calling by his surname, and his Christian name was Derek. She pinched the bottom of his neck quite hard at the side where it joined his body. Apparently, this was a spot that would sometimes wake someone up and make them open their eyes and come round, but not Derek

She stood by the bedside talking to us, and she said, "Don't worry. He is a very strong person. He will wake up when he is ready. Some people are like this for days, and when he comes round he will say some very funny things that will make you laugh.

I will pray for him tonight, as I pray for all my patients every night."

Then she said, "I must go and cook my babies a dinner."

She went on to tell us about her teenage children, and I said, "If they are teenagers, they should be cooking your dinner."

She laughed and said, "I know. I keep telling them that, but I still like to cook for them."

I asked her what time should she work until, and she told us twenty minutes ago, but she was prepared to stop and comfort us and talk to us instead of rushing home to her babies, as she called them, and we thought that was a lovely gesture on her part—a very dedicated lady.

If only we had gotten some response from him, that would have been the icing on the cake to be able to ring family and friends to tell them he was awake, talking, moaning, whatever. We took it in turns to go for a drink, but nobody would stay away for any length of time just in case he came round.

We were all reluctant to leave that night, but we had been at the hospital for several hours, and we needed to be alert for tomorrow, as we were sure tomorrow would be the day he would be awake.

Back home, we sat drinking our tea in the kitchen, relating the day's events. We agreed we were seeing a very small change in Derek now as each day passed. First, it was the very slight movement in his hand. The next day, his feet and legs moved, and today the yawning. It could only get better, as they say.

I felt a little more relaxed as I climbed in bed, but at the same time I could not help wondering when Derek did come round whether he will have any form of disabilities. Whatever, I will be there for him.

Once again, I asked Mum for her help. People perhaps think I'm silly, but since Mum lived with us for the last year of her life, I feel as though she's there for me.

I remember about three years ago—it was New Year's day. It was cold, and in the late afternoon Derek, lit a lovely fire so we could sit round it. We had decided to go abroad on holiday, and Derek had asked if our passports were still up to date. I knew where I usually had kept them, but when I went to look for them I could not find them and I searched for nearly three hours, in drawers, cupboards, handbags, books, you name it.

I looked and looked, and in the end I sat down on the bed and said, "Please, Mum, tell me where to look."

In less than ten minutes, something was telling me to look in the box where I had first thought they were. I got up and opened the box, and there in the very top of the box inside a cardboard wallet were the passports. They were still valid, and then I went and sat in front of the roaring fire. So, I'm sure she's with me now.

CHAPTER 8
Monday, March 26

We were all very excited this morning on the way to the hospital. Stuart and Caroline were in the front of the car laughing and saying, "I'll bet he'll be awake today."

When we arrived at the hospital and parked, we got out of the car, and all three of us rushed along, trying to get to the ward as quickly as we could. I was in front, as the other two were chattering away.

Stuart called out, "Steady, mother. Otherwise, you'll be the next one in here."

Caroline sat in the waiting room. As Stuart and I entered the ward, we were trying to peep round the curve of the ward to see if he was waiting for us, but as usual, we neared the bed and there he lay and had still not regained consciousness.

We were so disappointed. We kept talking to him, and we asked the nurse who was on duty if he had come round at all. She shook her head no. We could see at once he had had his hair washed again and the tube had been removed from his nose. We did not know whether this was a good sign or not. I went out after a while to let Caroline sit with Stuart, but shortly after, I decided to go back onto the ward. One of the nurses even bought a chair over from one of the beds so the three of us could sit down.

The bruising had almost disappeared on his face. There was a yellow tinge but nothing much and the swelling had almost gone, although his right eye lid was puffy.

Stuart had noticed a green colouring seeping through the bandage of his dad's operated hand and thought he could smell it, although he did not say anything to me at the time. He called the nurse over and asked her if his dad's hand was all right as he noticed the colour on the bandage and the smell. The young nurse laughed and said it was fine. They had tried feeding his dad with the liquid food through the tube, but it made him sick and it went all over his bandaged hand so they had to take the tube from his nose and stop feeding him until he was more alert. Stuart was relieved.

We watched monitors and the nurses changing the fluid bag, taking the boots from Derek's feet, and all the other general duties they had to do. The bandaged hand was still very swollen. The fingers that were visible were like fat sausages. Then, there was a slight movement in his good hand, but it was very slight and then nothing.

All the beds as you walked through the NCCU ward were on the left hand side. In the first bed was a teenage boy. You could only really see his mop of dark hair and his face was covered by tubes and wires and his bare chest was visible. Then, there were a couple of empty beds and then a lady was in the next bed propped up by pillows with an oxygen mask over her face. Other patients like Derek just lay there; some with visitors who only stayed a short time and then went because there was no response from their patient.

Derek's bed was the last one in a line, and then three beds went across the end wall with the bottom of each bed facing Derek's bed but three or four yards away from his bed. Then, like an alcove section joining the ward, were six beds, three each side facing one another and then swing doors on the end wall that were frequently used by members of staff. I later discovered this area was the high-dependency unit, which was a step closer to being put on a ward.

On each side of the corridor as you walked through the second set of double doors in the NCCU were small rooms where you could see patients lying in their beds, and sometimes you would see visitors putting on plastic aprons. Some had masks on and wore rubber gloves. I had no idea why these patients were separated from the main ward, but possibly to avoid infection from other visitors.

In the high-dependency unit, which adjoined the NCC ward, was a young girl of perhaps nine or ten. I assumed it was her grandfather sitting with her. Sometimes, he came on his own and other times with some other family members, but there was someone with her all the time, the same way we were at Derek's bedside. She sat watching television all day, and we thought this strange to be able to have television on in a critical-care ward but it was lovely to hear her laugh. When we first started coming to the ward, she would lay silent, but she appeared to be improving. The grandfather would disappear and then return with a mug of drink he had made himself in the visitors' kitchen.

The other patients in that section seemed to be in there a couple of days and then were moved or transferred elsewhere.

The nurse asked us to leave while they turned Derek, so we walked to the cafeteria. We decided to get a burger and some chips. We sat and ate them, and I had a cup of tea while the other two had a cold drink. Then, we wandered back to the ward. We thought if the nurses had moved him about, they would have woken him up, but, no, he was still out for the count.

Through the day, I kept repeating the words "Immaculate Heart of Mary, pray for us now and at the hour of our death".

When Gary and Anna arrived later, Stuart and Caroline went for a walk as they had been there all day and they left to give the other two a chance to sit with Derek. At this stage, I cannot remember whether they waited for us until home time or if they left and we met back home later, but all our hopes of Derek coming round that night were dashed. Later, we all sat round the table at home drinking tea and summarizing the day's events. Tomorrow was another day and hopefully would be more promising than today.

Perhaps the nurses washing his hair had tired him out, and he thought *I can't be bothered to open my eyes today.*

All sorts of things flood through your mind, but one always thinks in the end he is still with us and that means a lot.

CHAPTER 9
Tuesday, March 27

Stuart came out of the office this morning with a broad grin on his face. He had rang the hospital and spoken to the nurse in charge. The senior male nurse had told Stuart that although Derek was not awake, when he had taken hold of Derek's hand and asked Derek to squeeze it if he could hear and understand, Derek then squeezed his hand. What a brilliant way to start the morning!

"Right, Mother," Stuart said, "We'll just pop home and feed the pets, get ready, and we'll leave for the hospital as soon as we get back."

I rang Gary to give him the news, and he was delighted. He said he told me his dad would be all right. He said he would telephone a few friends and let them know that his dad had started to respond, however small that might be.

Sylv had called, and she was going to ring my other two sisters to tell them of the good news and also some of the Elvis team. She stopped with me until Stuart and Caroline had returned, and then off we went. Stuart had to stop and fill up at the petrol station as usual; then, they both went inside and got some sandwiches to eat en route. I just wished they would hurry up and get to the hospital.

We stood by the bedside, and I picked up Derek's hand and held it and spoke to him, "It's Chris. If you can you hear me, squeeze my hand."

Yes, there was slight pressure from his fingers on my hand. I wanted to cry. Stuart asked me to get out of the way because he wanted to see if he did the same to him, and he did. It was like winning the lottery—the jackpot at that.

The doctors did their ward rounds and approached the bed. After reading the notes, one of the doctors asked Derek to move his right foot, then his left foot, and then lift the left foot off the bed, then lift the right one up, which he did all of them very slightly. The doctors made notes and then went to the next bed.

Throughout the day at different times, we asked if he could hear us, did he know he was in hospital, if he knew Stuart's voice to squeeze his hand, and he did. He was also yawning a lot. He looked so funny when he did. He reminded me of a new-born baby yawning with a tiny mouth, and when his mouth was fully open, his tongue was pure white.

The nurse also said that Derek had had his hand redressed this morning, and it was healing nicely.

Then, his two sisters, Heather and Shirley, brother Colin, and brother-in-law Chris came to visit, and when we told them, they were delighted. We left them by Derek's bedside and went for a cup of tea. When we arrived back outside the ward, I left Stuart and Caroline while I went through to the ward, and his youngest sister said he had squeezed her hand also, when she asked some questions. So, they were also well chuffed.

I rang Gary from outside the hospital, and he said that he and Anna would be along later. By the time they arrived, they were both excited, and we took it in turns to sit with Derek. I mostly stayed by the bedside, but Stuart and Caroline would go for a walk to give Gary and Anna time to spend with Dad.

We got home all excited that something new had happened today. I felt so relieved there had been some response.

Stuart and Caroline left for an hour while they went home to feed the pets. Gary and Anna stayed with me until they arrived back. I kept telling them all to go home as I would be all right. I had both dogs to protect me, one inside the house and one outside, but they insisted on staying and not leaving me alone at any one stage, which was very kind of them all.

Gary went outside and put some wood on the burner. After then, we sat and chatted. He told me of the people who had rung his mobile asking after Derek. He then said they would come and visit tomorrow and then stay to bring me home tomorrow night. I also remembered that the bag Anna had packed with Derek's things in on the eve of his accident was still in the boot of the car. I had to remember to get it out in the morning, as how things were, it was no telling when he would need them and they would get damp in the car.

As soon as Stuart and Caroline came back, Gary and Anna left. I went upstairs for a shower and then came downstairs in my dressing gown to talk to them. After a while, I went to bed, wondering whether I would sleep as I was feeling much better tonight.

Perhaps tonight I would not worry as much that the telephone might ring during the night and a voice would say, "It's Addenbrookes hospital. Can you come? Derek's poorly."

Did the prayer that I kept repeating over the last couple days now begin to work? I hoped so. The heavy feeling I had had inside my chest all week had lifted. It was like a bottle of champagne had been uncorked inside me—all bubbly.

CHAPTER 10
Wednesday, March 28

Today, Stuart and Caroline would have to leave about one o'clock, but as we were standing by the bed, we saw it happen! A slight movement began, and Derek started to move about in the bed as though trying to get comfortable, moving his arms and legs about and half turning over. We kept talking to him. He was lying flat on his back. Then, I saw his eyes very slightly open and his head move very slowly, looking from one side to another.

I said, "Hello, Darling. You're in hospital. You've had a nasty fall from your truck."

He said, "Go and ask them. Go on. Grid reference 1144. They'll know."

He had seen a couple of nurses standing at the desk opposite his bed, and he was repeating this grid reference over and over again.

Stuart and I sat trying to guess what this grid reference meant.

Stuart said, "As soon as we get home, we'll look on the map and see if it's anything to do with Salisbury, where Dad was going to take his load."

Then, after a little while, Derek fell back into a deep sleep.

Before Stuart and Caroline left, I went to the cafeteria to have a drink and something to eat. As soon as I got back, they left for home. I sat hoping Derek would wake, but he didn't. I kept talking to him and then just sat and watched him for hours.

I asked the nurse what medication Derek was on, as they always seemed to be pumping something into the needle that was inserted in his hand. She told me that he was having antibiotics, paracetamol, calcium, and insulin, and I asked if they had discovered diabetes. She said the insulin was because his sugar levels would automatically drop, so it was to keep him stable. He also had an injection in his tummy to stop his blood from clotting. It's a good job he didn't know he was having all this medication, otherwise, I think he would refuse it all. He was still wearing his "sexy" knee-length plaster boots.

Two ladies came in and sat with a young lady in the far-end bed. You could see she had had an operation on her head, as nearly all her hair was shaven off and you could see the stitches. Soon after, they walked by the end of Derek's bed and smiled and spoke to me. I walked over to them, and they asked me how long had I been coming here? They wanted to know what had happened to Derek, so I told them the story of the accident.

The older lady then went on to tell me that her friend had driven her to the hospital as her daughter-in-law had been knocked over by a car as she was crossing the road, and her husband was a long-distance truck driver and was unable to get home right away. They stayed and chatted another ten minutes. They said they would most likely see me again, because she had been told that her daughter-in-law had very serious internal injuries as well and likely to be in hospital for a while but her husband would be here at the weekend. They both wished Derek all the best and left.

The bed that stood endways next to Derek had a coloured girl in her twenties, and she had a pretty face. She was lying asleep, and the nurses came and went after they had taken her temperature, blood pressure, and blood samples. She was connected to monitors, the same as Derek was, bleeping away. They would raise the head of the bed up a little and then later lower it. I could not help but see the comings and goings of the nurses attending to the other patients, because I was sitting to Derek's right-hand side of the bed and was facing some of the other patients.

Three coloured visitors walked by, and the man nodded to me and went to the young lady's bed. I assumed it was mother, father, and sister. I heard them singing a gospel song to her very softly. I could not hear the words, but it was a very moving scene. It actually bought tears to my eyes.

The curtains were then quickly closed around the empty bed behind me, and then a lot of commotion. There was obviously another patient being bought in. I noticed a shadow of someone near me, and when I looked up two ladies stood there.

They then went inside the curtains. Only fifteen minutes later, I heard loud sobbing through the curtain and both females comforting each other. They slowly walked to stand near the nurses' desk until they were taken away by a nurse. Not long after, all the curtains were drawn around all the beds in the room, and I could hear men's voices coming from the curtain behind me.

They had obviously lost their loved one. Although I had never seen them before and would never likely to see them again, my heart went out to them, I felt sick because that could have been me and my family.

The curtains were all drawn back again and the bed behind me was empty. Soon afterwards, two nurses came and stripped the sheets from the bed and then completely scrubbed and dried the mattress and cleaned every part of the bed. Later, they put on clean bed linen ready for the next patient.

Gary and Anna were disappointed when they arrived to find Derek still a sleep. Anna kept stroking Derek's arm and talking to him. I left them to go for a cup of tea. Fifteen minutes later, I returned, hoping Derek was awake, but still no response from him. We stayed until after eight o'clock, and the nurse who was looking after Derek said it didn't look like he was going to wake up, so we left, as the nurse said she was going to make him comfortable for the night.

I told Gary and Anna on the way home of the day's events on the ward, and they said perhaps dad would be more alert tomorrow.

After we arrived home, there were more get-well cards that had arrived in the post that morning with some lovely, touching messages inside, not only for Derek but for the whole family.

Gary went outside for a smoke and to make the wood burner up, and Anna and I sat talking. Once Gary came back in, I went up to bed. After having a shower, I climbed into bed and soon fell asleep clutching Derek's pillow.

CHAPTER 11
Thursday, March 29

As Caroline, Stuart, and I walked up to the bed this morning, Derek was sleeping, and we gave a little sigh. We thought he would be awake for us today. Possibly, we were being selfish. He must need the sleep. We did not know how much the drugs affected him, because Derek has never been on any before. They had knocked him out for the count.

After about ten minutes, he started to move about, and then he opened his eyes, looking about him as we started to talk to him. All of a sudden, he started to nod his head. It was amazing that he recognized us. It was a very emotional experience for all of us.

I felt as though I wanted to run outside and telephone everyone up to tell them.

We explained to him that he was in hospital after falling off his truck. Could he understand? He nodded.

The three of us kept talking and telling him of his injuries, about the dogs, telling stories about the grandchildren, how many times we had been to see him, so he knew exactly how long he had been asleep. He looked so bewildered lying there, not sure if he understood why he was in hospital.

Throughout the day, his left hand kept trying to reach the ventilator tube that was in his mouth in order to pull it out. He could get his hand up toward his mouth, but he had not got the strength to reach it and his hand would slide back down his body, pulling the sheet with his hand.

Stuart laughed and said to him, "Hi, Dad. You're showing your pubics" and we would laugh, but we got used to what his intensions were and kept moving his hand away from the ventilator and laying it back on the bed.

Then, one of the monitors kept bleeping, and the nurse walked over and put the clip back on his finger. You could see Derek using his thumb to push the clip off of his finger. This happened several times during the course of the day, but as soon as we heard the bleeping one of us would quickly put the clip back on his finger again.

I left Stuart and Caroline with him while I went to have something to eat and drink, which took about half an hour. When I got back to the ward, it was time for them to leave to pick the children up from school.

They said their goodbyes, and I said to Derek, "Give them a wave. They have to go," and he lifted up his hand a couple of inches off the bed covers and gave them a wave.

Oh boy! I had tears rolling down my cheeks. This was one giant leap for him.

He dozed off once or twice but not for long. He was more interested in where he was. He kept watching people walking back and forth. He mumbled a few words during the course of the day, but I could not understand them

When a nurse walked by, she smiled as much as to say "Oh, at last he is awake." The family that came to visit the coloured girl walked by, and the man gave the thumbs up sign and his brilliant white teeth shining as he smiled. I think visitors and staff had wondered like us, if or when would Derek wake.

I heard the telephone ring at the nurses' desk, and then someone called my name, "Mrs Russell, there's a call for you."

For a moment I couldn't think who would be calling me, then the nurse whispered, "It's your son."

I said, "Hello" and then heard Gary's voice.

He said, "Mum, I really don't feel very well today. I don't think I should come to the hospital. I've got a sore throat and the start of a cold, and I don't want to give it to Dad. I would willingly come and pick you up, but I don't want to give it to you so you are unable to visit Dad."

I told him not to worry, and I would see if Stuart would come back to pick me up. He and Caroline with the children drove back to Cambridge to collect me. When they arrived, Stuart and Caroline came to the side of the bed and were talking to their Dad. Stuart asked his dad if he could remember the nickname he had for Caroline, and Derek mumbled something. Stuart asked him again, and he replied, "Sugar Babe" and we all laughed.

Stuart said, "Hi, Dad, that's enough of that. That's my wife you're talking to." Derek always called Caroline "Pukka Fairy" because the first few weeks after we had met Caroline, she would use the word "pukka" a lot in conversation. And then, New Year's Eve, when they had the children, they had a party and she had made the children fancy-dress costumes to wear. She and Stuart got into the party spirit, and Stuart dressed as Elvis and Caroline as a fairy in a tight pink fairy dress. When Derek found out, he immediately called her a "Pukka Fairy," and it has always stuck.

I left them by the bedside and went and sat in the car with the children so Caroline and Stuart had a little while with Derek. Gaby was twelve-years-old and a very sensible girl, and the boys were nine and six. They sat in the car, playing various games on their Nintendo. Just before it was time to leave, Caroline came back to be with the children while I went back to the ward to kiss Derek goodnight.

Gary had been worried about me sleeping alone in the house that night, but since Derek was more responsive, I really did not mind.

I was really happy and wondered whether I would get to sleep. When I arrived home, I opened some more get-well cards. Although they were addressed to Derek, I read them and intended taking them to the hospital to show him once he was well enough to look at them.

I guessed I should go to bed as the morning would soon arrive, and I knew tomorrow would be another long day. I was tired after all; as soon as I climbed into bed, I could not remember anything until morning.

CHAPTER 12
Friday, March 30

Stuart and Caroline were taking me this morning, and then it was their turn to have the children for the weekend, so they would only be able to stay at the hospital for a short while. We entered the ward and saw Derek—although he was asleep, he had the ventilator removed earlier that morning and he was now wearing an oxygen mask. We started to talk to him, and he stirred and slightly opened his eyes to see who was there. Then, he tried to pull the mask from his mouth, which he did several times during the course of the day.

I sat there talking to him, but he just nodded or whispered yes. I just had a gut feeling he really didn't know who I was or what I was talking about. Stuart and Caroline left and once again I was on my own, but that did not bother me at all.

While the nurses made him more comfortable, I walked to the cafeteria for my usual cup of tea and a salad. As I walked back to the ward, I met a mother with her daughter or daughter-in law and her husband. They were making their way to where I had come from. We had seen each other before while entering the ward, and one day, I had held the door open for them and exchanged a thank you. The older lady made eye contact with me, and we gave each other a smile, knowing we had patients in the same ward.

When I arrived back at the side of the bed, I noticed Derek's mask had disappeared and inserted in each nostril was a small oxygen tube. The nurse explained that he just kept pulling the mask off, so they had to find another solution to stop him.

He kept licking his lips, and I asked the nurse if he could have anything to drink, but she said no. However, she returned with a mouth swab and a cup with mouth wash in it. From the faces he pulled when the nurse wiped the inside of his mouth and lips, he really did not like it. I asked if I could go to the shop and buy a sweet lolly on a stick for him to suck, and she said she was sure that would be ok as long as he did not bite pieces off the lolly and choke.

I laughed and said, "What? With no teeth in his mouth?"

In the shop, I brought a selection of sweet lollies and bars of lemon-flavoured toffee. As I made for the doors to the critical-care unit, there stood the older lady of the two who I had met and smiled at earlier along the corridor. She had pressed the bell and was waiting for someone to open the doors. We exchanged a few words, saying who we had on the ward and how long they had been in hospital, when we heard the door make a clicking sound and knew we could enter the ward.

I arrived back at the bed and took out a children's-size bar of lemon toffee and just put it against Derek's lips. Once he got the taste of it, he really enjoyed it, but after he had been sucking it a little while it became very soft and I was afraid he would suck a piece off and choke. I wrapped that up and put it in the bag. I waited until he started to lick his lips again later on and then took out a small, sweet, strawberry lolly, which he had to suck on. After a few seconds, he shook his head as he obviously did not want anymore.

While dozing on and off, he kept repeating this grid reference over and mumbling things I could not understand, but I just kept talking to him and agreeing with him. During the day, I watched the nurses busy doing their tasks on their shift: walking around their patient's bed, checking monitors, and recording notes on the bedside charts. Nurses would assist each other with patients that needed turning. Doctors came and walked through the ward, some I had seen on previous days, others were strangers. Nurses would change shifts, and the nurse that was going to change over would come on duty ten or fifteen minutes before hand and go through the charts and day's events with the nurse that was then going off duty.

Gary was still feeling poorly and Caroline and Stuart had the children, so I rang to see if Derek's mate, Mike, would come and pick me up. When he arrived, he sat five minutes with Derek talking to him, but Derek just mumbled on and we could not make sense of anything he said. Shortly after, he went into a deep sleep so we left him to settle down for the night.

I felt sorry for Mike, as he had left off work and drove straight to the hospital without having a meal, but he seemed quite happy that he was able to see Derek. He had wanted to come and see him the night he was admitted to hospital, but one of the Elvis team advised him not to, as at that time no one knew what the situation was. We had a giggle in the car park as I insisted on paying the parking fee as Stuart had taken the two-week parking ticket home with him. Mike insisted he wanted to pay, so off he went to the parking machine while I walked to his car. A few minutes later, he came running back and asked if I had any change, as he didn't have enough on him. Once that was sorted, we left for home. I was giving him directions, but he missed the left turning at the traffic lights and went straight ahead, so we had to continue along the road until we came to another roundabout a mile or so ahead to come back to find the road we should have turned down. I had had a good day, so I felt I deserved a laugh.

Home at last, but I was looking forward to tomorrow. I hoped to sleep like a log and awake refreshed to begin another day.

CHAPTER 13
Saturday, March 31

Stuart, Caroline, and the children arrived to take me to the hospital. There was a lot of traffic on the road, so I suggested taking a shortcut through Queen Adelaide that would bring us out at the Ely roundabout, missing quite a bit of the slow-moving traffic, but instead of directing him straight over the staggered junction, I told Stuart to turn right and we ended up going through Ely city centre. It seemed as though everyone was out shopping. It was a very busy little place. I had been there on a couple of occasions, but a very long time ago. Several cars were queuing at the traffic lights and pedestrians all over the place, but the young grandsons got to see a fancy Lamborghini sports car. It looked very smart—painted bright yellow—standing on the side of the road, so it was worth missing our turning to hear their comments on it.

Here we were again, back at the hospital, very excited today. We left Gaby with the boys while Stuart and Caroline came with me to see Derek, but he was just the opposite of what he had been like the day before. He just lay there asleep.

Stuart was disappointed not seeing his dad awake. They were going to take the children out over the weekend, so I suggested that they leave to spend time with them, as they had spent so much time at the hospital since Derek's accident. Stuart and

Caroline had obviously missed spending time with the children, and it was only fair for them to spend more time together, as children don't always understand the situation.

As I sat by the bedside, the ward doctor came and stood by the bed with a nurse and a smartly dressed man in a grey, pin-striped suit. I discovered later he was one of the neurology surgeons; he just nodded his head to me and then started to speak to the ward doctor. I heard him say that another scan was needed to see what was going on in Derek's head as something must have happened since he was not responding to us at all.

I walked to the bottom of the bed and approached the surgeon. I explained that Derek was awake and talking most of the day before, and I asked if he could have tired himself out.

The neurosurgeon replied, "Nonsense. He should be more alert today than what he was yesterday. He needs another scan."

And then, he walked off to the next bed. Ten or fifteen minutes later, the nurse said they were going to take Derek for a scan and why didn't I go for a cup of tea. They would be back in an half an hour or so.

Sitting having a cup of tea, I wondered what the result of the scan would be. Had he starting bleeding inside his head again? All sorts of things go through your mind, and I kept looking at my watch. At times, it seemed as though it had stopped. I slowly made my way back to the ward and recognised faces from previous days, either on the ward or from sitting in the cafeteria. When I arrived back to the ward, the curtains were round Derek's bed, and I stood for a moment waiting for the curtains to be drawn back when a nurse peeped her head round and said you can come in if you like. They were making Derek more comfortable, and then they were gone. A few moments later, the nurse that was looking after Derek reappeared and whispered that the scan was OK. What a relief.

As I sat miles away thinking all different kind of thoughts, the ward doctor appeared by the bed.

He looked at me and said, "The scan was OK and nothing else has happened, but we think he has pneumonia and that is why he's so sleepy. I am going to arrange for the portable X-ray machine to come on the ward."

I wanted to cry, because I had read in the paper that if someone has a fall and after a few days, pneumonia sets in, then they pass away. I felt so sick, and there was no one there to talk to. The man with the X-ray machine appeared and asked me to stand over by the nurse's desk, because of the radiation. It only took a couple of minutes, and as he walked by me, I asked how long it would be before they knew the result. He replied about ten minutes. I sat on the chair once again by the bed, just as Derek's sister, her husband, and daughter walked in. I tried to tell them what had happened without crying, but I did not succeed. We sat talking and they stayed with me for a couple of hours. The nurse came to look at all the machines and check monitors. I asked her if she knew the result of the X-ray, but she said she did not know. I kept watching every time I heard footsteps, thinking it would be the doctor coming round to tell me the result. The sooner Derek was treated for the condition, the more likely his chance of him recovering from it. It was about five o'clock when I spoke to Derek, and at last, he answered me.

I telephoned Stuart to tell him of the news the doctor had told me. He could not believe it and said to ring him if I heard any more information.

Gary and Anna arrived to see their dad and stayed until it was time to take me home. Still no one had told us the results of that X-ray. As we walked out, I saw another nurse and asked her. She apologised but could not tell me anything, and there were no doctors around to ask.

I really felt deflated that night. We arrived home and went inside to have a cup of tea, Gary did the usual chore of making the wood burner up for me while I let Sally out, and she was mooching about. Once we were back inside, Gary and Anna left for home, so I made another cup of tea and took it upstairs to bed with me. As I lay there, I asked Mum to help Derek. Nothing could stop the tears from flowing. Then, I had a headache, and sleep would not come. I kept thinking the phone was going to ring in a minute telling us to get to the hospital. I must have finally dropped off but was awake early next morning.

CHAPTER 14
Sunday, April 1

Again, I was up early this morning. Sylv called round as usual, and then she went home for her usual dish of porridge. I was doing some odd jobs to keep my mind occupied when the phone rang, and it was Stuart to tell me he had rang the hospital and said Dad had had a comfortable night. I asked if they said about his X-rays, and he said the nurse did not know. So, after chatting for a few minutes, I put down the receiver and went back into the kitchen, when the telephone rang again. It was a friend who owned land next door to our house, and he always called on a Sunday morning to have a chat with Derek and they both used to put the world to rights over a cup of coffee. He asked if it was all right to pop in, so I boiled the kettle, and as he parked the car outside I made him a coffee. His first question was how Derek was. I tried to tell him without getting upset, but I just couldn't. I started crying and that made him upset as well. We were a right pair, sitting opposite each other. He stayed with me for about an hour and then left. I then got myself ready, as my brother Mick and his wife, Shirley, came to pick me up and take me to the hospital today.

We chatted away on the journey, but my mind was not really into the conversation. I kept wondering about what condition we would find Derek in that day and hoping they had started his antibiotics if he had gotten pneumonia.

As we walked along the corridor to the critical care unit I felt sick. What was I going to find when we got in there?

As we neared the bed, I could see Derek was a sleep, but I began talking to him, saying to him come on and wake up since Mick and Shirley have come to see you today. Although he did not open his eyes, he mumbled something. A nurse was sitting at her desk writing notes, and I asked if she knew anything about Derek's X-ray.

She shook her head and said, "No, sorry, no one has said anything."

Mick began talking to Derek but no response. Then I said, "Derek," and he answered, "What?"

I said, "Can Mick borrow the hedge cutter?"

He whispered, "Yes."

I knew where the hedge cutter was kept, but I asked him if it was in the garage.

Derek replied, "No."

I said, "Is it in the tool shed?"

He said, "Yes."

Then again I said, "Derek."

He replied, "What?"

"Can Mick borrow the chain saw?"

He again whispered, "Yes."

Once again, I was just testing him as I knew where it would be kept.

I said, "Is it in the garage?"

He said, "No."

"Derek, is it in the tool shed?"

He said, "Yes."

After a few minutes, I once again said, "Derek."

And then came an angry, "*What?*"

"Can Mick borrow the garden fork?"

He answered, "Yes," and then he turned over and never said any more to us.

It had caused a laugh as I think Mick had asked to borrow most things in that half an hour from the workshop to try and keep Derek in a conversation, but the last reply of "*What!*" was very angry. As much as to say "for Christ sake, shut up and leave me alone."

As Mick and Shirley left, I walked down to the cafeteria for a drink and something to eat and then returned to the ward. Derek was back into a sound sleep.

It was about four o'clock when I noticed the very doctor from the previous day who had thought Derek had gotten pneumonia. He came walking along the middle of the ward, as staff could walk through the same doors as we came through and walk right through the ward and exit by another set of doors at the opposite end.

I thought he was coming toward me, but he was looking down at some notes and I knew he was going to go straight by, so I stepped out in front of him and said, "Doctor, has Derek got pneumonia?"

He just looked at me and said, "No. The X-rays were fine" and walked off.

Although I was very relieved, I also felt very angry that the family had spent twenty-four hours thinking the worst. I had had a sleepless night, and no one had had the decency to let me know that the X-ray results were OK.

I couldn't wait for Stuart and Caroline to arrive to give them the good news. I spent another couple of hours just sitting watching the world go by—well in the ward anyway. I had a book with me and opened it and started to read, but I kept reading the same words over and over again, so I closed the book and put it back in my handbag.

The man sat by the bed of his wife, who had been knocked down. He was looking very uneasy, so I decided to walk over to him for a chat. I told him to have faith and not to give up. He asked all about Derek's injuries, and after a while I left him and went back to Derek's bedside. When he left later, he nodded and said, "Thank you."

The Three Birds

A nurse walked by and then came back with a small television and set it up on Derek's small table at the foot of the bed. I asked what was the idea of that, and she said once the patient has started to respond, it can help to stimulate the brain. The nurse left it switched on and walked off.

A wildlife programme started, and then Derek turned over, opened his eyes and began watching it. He mumbled a couple of times.

Just then, Stuart and Caroline walked in the ward, and Stuart said, "What? Have they supplied you with a television, now?" but he was completely surprised to see his dad actually watching it.

Derek was watching a documentary on meerkats at the time, and then it went on to tigers, lions, and cheetahs. He kept saying how marvellous they were and they were the fastest animal, and we realized he was making a lot of sense.

After the wildlife programme ended, Stuart said that Gaby would like to come in and see Granddad, but asked if Granddad would like to see Gaby, and Derek's eyes lit up and he nodded his head up and down and whispered, "Yes."

So, off Stuart and Caroline went. Caroline would stay in the car with the boys, and Stuart would bring Gaby in the ward. Before they entered the ward, Stuart made Gaby aware of all the machine bleeping and that some patients would look very poorly, but she understood that if she did not like it she would go back to the car. But Gaby and Granddad talked away, although it was a job for Gaby to understand Granddad at times. We deciphered the words where we could. Granddad was asking about school and the boys. This was the first time we could see a light at the end of the tunnel.

Gaby then went back and sat in the car with the boys while Caroline came back to have ten minutes with Derek before they left, as Gary and Anna were coming to pick me up.

Gary was amazed at the improvement he could see in his dad. They must have been there about an hour when two nurses arrived at the bedside and asked if we would mind leaving, because they wanted to move Derek to the High Dependency Unit. We said we would leave, and I asked where I could find Derek tomorrow.

The nurse smiled and said, "Oh, in here but closer to the door."

I turned and looked across the ward and saw a space right next to the door. So visiting time would be just the same—any time—and the nurse smiled and said, "Of course." I also asked if the television would be going with Derek, and she said it would. We said our goodbyes and told Derek we would see him tomorrow. Although I was very relieved he was able to talk, I was sad that he now knew where he was. Since he was alert, it would be worse for him.

On the way home, Gary rang family and friends to say that Derek was bright and cheerful and being moved, although not a great distance but it was another step forward and out of the critical-care unit.

I felt I could go to bed tonight and relax a little more, knowing tomorrow would not be as stressful as the past days had been.

CHAPTER 15
Monday, April 2

I was up early and felt refreshed. I had a brilliant night's sleep. I showered, dressed, switched the kettle on, let the dog out, went across to make the boiler up, and then came back and made a cup of tea and sat and enjoyed it for the first time. I suddenly remembered that the television the nurse had bought Derek to watch, had a slot at the bottom for videos, so I went to the unit where the videos were kept and opened the drawer to select some to take to the hospital. In these two drawers Derek kept Second World War stories, all documentaries, which he had always been very interested in. I chose one on war and one on different aircraft used in the war, and then I opened the other drawer to find the story of F1 motor racing by Murray Walker. It is the only sport Derek really likes. He hates football and cannot understand why a gang of men want to chase a bag of wind around in all weathers. If he happen to turn the television on and a football match was on and it was pouring rain he would always say, "I bet if you asked the buggers to go outside to work in it, they wouldn't do it." He would listen sometimes to Wimbledon on the radio in the truck, but has never really been interested watching it on the television. I would also take a video of one of his own Elvis concerts to watch and just see his reaction.

The telephone rang, and it was a man from the health and safety department, who had rang to see how Derek was and to explain that no way was the timber frame company that had hired Derek to haul wooden floor sections to Salisbury was at fault for Derek's accident. It was Derek who used the wooden sections as a ladder, therefore the case was closed.

My sister June and her husband John were taking me this morning, so I was excited and could not wait to get there. It did not seem such a long journey this morning. I knew it was the same distance, but I just felt better and more relaxed knowing Derek was improving day by day.

As we walked through the ward, we could not see Derek as his bed was around the corner of the ward. On reaching him, he was sitting in a high-backed, leather-type chair, slumped over, and then I heard my sister gasp, and say, "OH, Derek," with a quiver in her voice. His face was white and his part-shaven head looked awful. The doctor had removed the pressure-release monitor from his head, so the baldness was more prominent. His hand still had the Scholl like support on it, and his fingers were still very swollen. They were upset to see him like that, but I was over the moon.

We sat talking to him, but he just kept replying yes or no in an almost whisper or just nodding his head very slowly. You could see he had lost an awful lot of weight, and it was so unlike Derek to be sitting so still. We sat talking to each other as well, so Derek could just sit and listen as he did not seem interested.

I could smell food odours wafting through the doors when a young male nurse appeared, and I asked him if Derek could eat anything as yet. He replied that he could not give Derek any food until the speech therapist had come and tested his throat, because the head injury might have affected his throat muscles. So, I asked if I could try him with some food. He went and asked another member of staff and came back and said I could try him with some. I could not really see what difference it made whether a nurse fed Derek or I did. I asked what was there for him to eat. The nurse came back with a plate of mashed potato and white fish, so I mashed a small piece of fish into some potato and started to feed Derek. After about three forkfuls, he shook his head. When the nurse came back in to see if Derek was feeding OK, he said if he doesn't want any more he'd take it away, and would I like to try him with some custard. Back he came with a dish of custard, and I started to feed Derek. He enjoyed it, but once again after a few spoonfuls he did not want anymore.

 He kept trying to move in the chair, and I asked if he was uncomfortable and he nodded. When the nurse came back through the doors, I asked him if Derek could go back to bed as he was really fidgety. He said he would go and get some help. When he returned with another nurse, they asked us to leave while they made Derek more comfortable and put him to bed. I told Derek I would be back after I have had a cup of tea.

 The three of us walked from the ward in silence. I then asked June what she thought of Derek.

 She said, "Oh, Chris, I would never have recognised him if you had not been with us. He looks so poorly."

 She told me to come and sit in their car because she had made some sandwiches and a flask of drink, and I had explained to her how the cafeteria was always full of staff around lunch time, it was also very noisy. I had learnt not to go for some lunch until after one p.m., when there would be more tables available and I liked to sit on my own to think.

 After they had left to travel back home, I went back to the ward. Derek was fast asleep, so I sat and again just watched him. He had about an hour's sleep when he woke and I took hold of his hand and began talking to him. Then, I remembered the videos I had put in his locker, so without asking him I switched the television on and put in a war documentary film. He never took his eyes off it. He was like a baby when you switch the television on and sit them in front of it to keep them amused while you got on with some work.

 Because it was giving him some interest, when that one had finished, I put another one on, as the ones I had brought where only about forty-five minutes long so he would not get fed up too soon. The nurses where backwards and forwards and smiling each time they went by.

When the second video had finished, I ask Derek if he would like to watch a Grand Prix—one of the Murray Walker highlights, like the worst car crashes during a race—and we both sat watching it when Derek all of a sudden said, "Keep watching, keep watching—one of his wheels will fly off in a minute."

Sure enough, within a few seconds it did, and I was amazed that Derek could remember that clip in the film footage. It gave me more hope than ever to think he could remember that.

It was tea time, and the nurse came in to see if Derek would like some tea. She had some vegetable soup or sandwiches. I thought the soup would be better, so she left it, and again I fed him. He had a couple of coughs during the meal, but I knew there was someone close by if I should need help if he started to choke. He did not eat all the soup, and again I asked if they had any custard. The nurse returned with some custard, so I began feeding him with that, but he soon had had enough and shook his head. At least that's a start; at least he was beginning to eat. There was a long way to go but in the right direction.

The boys came to visit their dad at night, and Derek started to ramble on a bit and was making everyone laugh, mainly because we could not understand what he was saying, so tonight I was yet again relieved at the improvement Derek has made.

CHAPTER 16
Tuesday, April 3

I was up, dressed, and ready to go. I had answered several phone calls and did not mind who I spoke to now, as I knew Derek was out of danger. Keith was round to walk the dogs; Sylv had already left; and I had spoken to one of Derek's sisters.

Derek's sister's husband, Chris, was taking me to the hospital this morning, as he was a rep on the road everyday and was in the Cambridgeshire area so it worked out just right. He took a completely different route to the way I normally went to Addenbrookes Hospital, and I enjoyed the scenery. Don't ask me which way he had gone, but I thought we were ending up at Cambridge airport as that was where the signs kept pointing to, but then we headed straight by there and came into Addenbrookes Hospital from a different way. It didn't matter how I got there, as long as I did.

I was getting used to the journey now but did keep wondering how long Derek would be here for? I was dropped off outside the back entrance to the hospital, which I knew like the back of my hand, as that's where we parked the car on a daily basis. I quickly made my way to the ward, and Derek was sitting in the chair at the side of the bed. He still looked very white and lifeless. I gave him a kiss, but I don't think he knew who I was. I sat talking to him about the dogs and all the people who had enquired about him, but he never really replied to any of it, just kept saying, "Oh." I asked him if he wanted to watch television, and he said, "If you like," but there was nothing much on, so I put one of his Elvis concert videos on. He sat staring at it. Every time a nurse went by they stopped to watch it for a few minutes and then realized it was Derek, but I don't think he even knew it was himself he was watching. I gave him some soup for lunch, followed by some custard. Once again, I could see he was uncomfortable. He tried moving, but just seemed as though he hadn't got the strength to move, so when a nurse came by I asked if Derek could lie down for a while.

She smiled and said, "I'll get someone to help me."

Soon after, two nurses came to the bedside and asked me leave while they put Derek back to bed.

I walked to the shop and purchased my ready-made salad. I chose a chicken salad and found a table in the corner to sit and eat it. It was a little bit quieter today. There were still several members of staff eating their lunch but not so hectic as some days. After I had eaten my salad, I made my way to the other side of the room where I could help myself to a cup of tea from the machine and a chocolate-covered muffin. As I stood waiting to pay at the till, I looked up, and on the opposite side queuing to pay for his lunch, was a coloured doctor who I had seen on the ward probably only once or twice. He smiled, showing lovely white teeth, and he asked how my husband was, which I thought was a lovely gesture. I replied that he was doing much better and had started to eat. His reply was that was good and take care. He paid for his food and left. After I had paid for my things I found another table close by to sit and drink my tea, but I couldn't wait to get back to the ward.

Nick was on duty today, and he always found time to come and talk to me. He never did stop for long, but that did not matter as he was organizing other members of staff.

He disappeared through the swing doors and about five minutes later came over to the bed and said, "Elvis, we are going to move you onto a ward upstairs. We've had enough of you here," and laughed. "No," he said, "you can be moved now; you are off the critical list."

So, we gathered up his belonging and put them on the bed, and with Nick at the top end of the bed and a nurse holding the folder with all Derek's notes in one arm and the other hand guiding the bed, round the corner we went into the corridor by the lift. Next to the lift were the doors that I walked through daily into the NCCU.

The lift doors opened and the bed was pushed in, and I followed. The doors closed, and we moved slowly upwards. Nick had a laugh with Derek and told him he would pop up to see him sometime. Within seconds, the lift had stopped, and the doors opened and we walked from the lift through a set of doors opposite and along a dark corridor, past rooms with patients lying in bed. Then Nick stopped against the nurses' desk, exchanged paperwork and conversation, and then Derek was pushed into a smaller room behind the nurses' station to a space beside the window. Nick and the nurse left us. I thought at least he's near the window and he can look out, but how wrong I was, as I turned and looked out to see only the roof of another building. You could see the clouds if you looked up high enough. Cambridge airport was nearby, and occasionally you could see an aeroplane fly over. I know it was another step of improvement, but the critical-care ward was so light and airy and so spacious compared to this ward.

The sister came in and introduced herself and said a nurse would be along to take some details. She walked away and came back with a chair, which Derek was to sit in to be weighed. I was shocked that within just over two weeks he had lost three stone—yes, three stone. That was one good reason why he did not have the strength to even talk.

There were six beds in the ward, three each side, and they were all occupied. The other patients were asleep after they had had small operations on their heads, or they were just lying there. There were no other visitors in the room. Soon after the nurse came and sat down by the bed and asked all the usual details, I asked if visiting times were the same, and she replied visiting was 10.30 a.m. until 1.00 p.m., then 2.30 p.m. until 8.00 p.m.

After she left, I told Derek I would not be able to come so early tomorrow, but I don't think he knew what I was talking about. I heard a lot of clattering outside the ward and could smell food. Just afterward, a young, coloured nurse went to the patient just inside the room at the end bed with a plate of food and started feeding the man. She looked up and smiled, so I asked her if Derek was going to have a meal.

She replied, "Yes, but I can only feed one patient at a time, and I have four wards to look after."

I said that I could feed Derek if she would like me to, and she was really pleased.

She said, "When I have finished giving this man his food, I will get you some food for your husband."

True to her word, she was soon back with a plate of potato, mince, and vegetables covered in gravy. I really mashed everything together because I had noticed Derek coughed now and again when he swallowed anything, so I had to be careful not to choke him. After a few mouthfuls, he shook his head and said no more. He had also got some crumble with custard, and I fed him with that. His cup of tea was in a plastic mug with a straw, and I waited for it to cool as he never did like a hot drink.

I would drink mine, and he would say, "God, have you drunk yours already?"

I sat watching him, wondering what he must be thinking—with his swollen hand in cast, a catheter fitted at the front, and a tube inserted in his rear end—to wake up and find all this apparatus in him and not know how or why. I told him I would have to go and telephone Gary to let him know which ward he was in and what room, so I left him and walked down the corridor, through the cafeteria and shops, and outside so I could use my mobile. I explained to Gary, and he said he was about to leave so he would be with me in an hour. I said

I would walk back down to the car park and meet him, so we could walk back together.

Derek just sat there staring into space. I sat talking to him about our dogs and neighbours, etc., but he still only answered with a yes or no. There was no conversation because he did not know who I was talking about. He closed his eyes as much as to say he could not be bothered to listen anymore, so I let him rest. I just sat watching the odd aeroplane fly over from or to the airport. You could not watch it for long because the tall rooftop of the building next to the window obscured almost all the sky. You heard the plane and then caught a glimpse of it as it passed by. I thought how nice it would have been for Derek if he could have watched the world go by from the window, but there it could not have been helped. He was there to be nursed and looked after. I glanced at my watch and decided to go for a walk to the car park and wait for Gary.

I had been standing there about five minutes when I saw Gary walk across the car park and smile as he approached me. "How's it going, then, Mother" were always Gary's first words, and he gave me a kiss. I told him of the day's events, and when we got to the ward, Derek still had his eyes closed. Gary tried to make a conversation with him to no avail.

We sat talking between ourselves, and Gary said, "This isn't as nice a ward as the critical care, but I suppose that ward has to be so bright and clean and spacious and this room is smaller and everything closer together."

The telephone at the nurses' desk was constantly ringing, and one patient from another ward was constantly wandering about. She walked in the ward a couple of times, and a nurse followed her and took her back out again to the ward she belonged to. Soon after, the end-of-visiting-time bell sounded, and we had to leave. I leaned forward and told Derek we would have to leave, and he just mumbled something. He did not even open his eyes. Perhaps the move from one ward to another had upset him. I didn't know. Perhaps tomorrow—just perhaps—he might be more cheerful.

CHAPTER 17

Wednesday, April 4

My niece, Sue, was taking me to the hospital today, along with my two sisters, Joyce and Sylv. I gave her instructions how to get to the hospital, and when we arrived there, we all went onto the ward. I saw a nurse and asked if the four of us could sit round Derek's bed as we had driven from King's Lynn.

She said, "I'm sorry; only two visitors at a time."

So Joyce and Sylv went to have a cup of tea while Sue and I went to see Derek. He was sitting in the chair by the side of the bed, and we told him Joyce and Sylv were having a cup of tea and asked if he would like to go downstairs and see them. He nodded "yes", so I found a nurse and asked if I could take him to see my other two sisters. She said she would find a wheelchair for us to push him in. While we were waiting, I realized that the food tube up his nose had disappeared. He had had one inserted a few days ago because he was still not eating enough.

When the nurse came to the bedside, I asked when they had taken it out.

She said, "We never. Derek pulled it out last night, so we will leave it out, as he has now started to eat solids and we will see how it goes."

She laughed and said that he had also pulled out the tube that was in his back passage, so I laughed and said he must have had a spring clean. I had noticed that his finger nails had been cut very short, and his fingers were stained an orangey brown colour as though it was nicotine stain, so that answered the question of why they were like that.

It was a very upright chair with wheels on, just like the those that porters used to ferry patients back and forth. The nurse helped Derek into the chair and put his urine bag on his lap and told him we must not forget his handbag. The nurse said she would find us a blanket to cover him up. She soon returned with a faded, blue blanket, which she covered over his legs and handbag (catheter bag), then off we went. The chair had solid wheels on it, and was a bit rough going. As we turned into the entrance to the sitting area, we spotted Joyce and Sylv sitting on seats nearest to us, so I pushed Derek up to them. They were already drinking a cup of tea, and since Derek only touched coffee at home, Sue went and got two cups of coffee and a tea for me. I had to leave Derek's coffee to get cooler before I dare give him any. I held the cup to his lips, and when he had a sip or two he started coughing.

He said, "I don't want anymore," and then he asked if I was taking him home.

This was the first time he had mentioned home, and from then on I knew he was beginning to feel better.

Joyce and Sylv were trying to make him laugh and join in the conversation, but once again I had my doubts as to whether he even knew who they were. He nodded now and again and even grinned a time a two, but had very little to say. Joyce told him he had to start putting some weight back on.

After about an hour, I asked him if he wanted to go back to the ward and he nodded, so Sue helped me push him back. Then, she would take the others home. You could see he had had enough, and his head was beginning to droop forward as though he hadn't got the strength to hold it upright.

Sue left, and I asked Derek if he wanted to lie down for a while. He said he did. I asked if he had a headache, and he whispered, "Yes," so I asked the nurse if he could have some painkillers. She said she would find out and after about five minutes came back and told Derek to swallow them. Once he had settled down, he turned over and went sound asleep. When he did stir, he kept trying to move in the bed, and I asked him what was the matter.

He replied, "I'm so sore. Just look for me, it hurts so much."

I asked if he meant his bum and he nodded, so I pulled the curtains around his bed and pulled his pyjama trousers down. The cheeks of his bottom were really red, although the skin was not broken.

I walked to the nurses' station and explained that Derek's bottom was red and he complained it was sore. I asked if they had any cream I could use. The nurse went to a large cupboard and came back with a tube of cream. The nurse came with me to look at area that was red, but said it was not too bad. I told her I would apply the cream as she was busy with some paperwork.

When the nurse had left, I said to Derek, "Here comes Nurse Russell on duty until eight o'clock."

No smile from him—he just said, "Yes."

Once I applied the cream, he dozed off again until Gary and Anna made an appearance. Although he never made much conversation with them, they were able to talk to him, and at least he answered them.

When we were ready to leave, I leaned over to give him a kiss goodnight, and he said, "Can't I come with you?"

I said. "I wish you could come home. It won't be long before you will, 'cause we've got a lot to catch up on."

Gary and Anna were pleased at the progress Derek had made. It was really the first time they could sit and talk to him, and he had actually answered them, perhaps only yes or no, but that was something. So I suppose it was another step in the right direction.

He had a very long way to go yet, and as he did not like hospitals. Once he was feeling better it would not surprise me if he did not discharge himself.

If only he was in a hospital closer to home, more people could go and see him to try and brighten up his day. After all, he must get fed up with me sitting constantly at his bedside, and it was a job to find different things to talk about as I was at the hospital all day as well.

Hopefully, once he started to get his strength back and began to walk about he would soon be home.

CHAPTER 18
Thursday, April 5

I woke early this morning and for the first time felt like tiding up and did some washing. I hoped I would be able to get things dry and ironed before I went to the hospital. Keith called and had a chat before going off with the dog

My sister, June, and her husband, John, were taking me today, and it was a cold day but dry and sunny. Of course, the hospital car park was busy because we were much later in the day, and there were several outpatient clinics. We walked inside the hospital, and there were quite a few people sitting drinking tea or coffee. We made our way to the ward, and there were a lot of people waiting by the lifts. I think there were three lifts on each side, kind of back to back. We only had a few stairs to climb, so decided we would walk up them.

We walked along the corridor until we got to the nurses' desk and walked behind into the ward. There was Derek lying down in bed with his back to the door. I walked round the side of the bed nearest the window and leaned over and spoke to him, but he did not answer. John then walked over to get a couple of chairs, and he and June sat on the opposite side of the bed to me. We kept talking amongst ourselves and were trying to get Derek to join in, but apart from moving his feet a couple of times, he just laid there as quiet as a mouse.

After an hour or so, June and John decided they would leave, so I walked with them to the shop area, so as they would not lose their way out. I had walked it so many times I could have done it with my eyes closed. It was then I decided to have a cup of tea with them, so, while they sat at a table, I went over to the machine and filled three polystyrene cups up with water. The tea bags were already inside the cups and sugar and milk stood on a tray beside the machine. We sat chatting as to why Derek had not spoken. Perhaps he had had a sleepless night and he was tired, or did he just feel poorly.

After they had left, I walked back to the ward, and Derek was still in the same position. I leaned over him and started to brush my fingers over his forehead. When he moved, I asked if he had a headache, and he very slowly nodded "yes". I went to the nurses' desk and asked if Derek could have something for a headache. The nurse said she would come and get Derek's chart from the bottom of the bed, which she did, so she could see when he had any medication and what time. She was soon back with two painkillers, and between us we managed to sit Derek up enough for him to swallow the tablets. Then, he slipped back down on the pillow. He never even opened his eyes or uttered a word, he just went back to sleep.

I had noticed that he had not worn his plaster-cast boots since he had been moved to that ward, so I thought this is a good opportunity to ask the nurse why this was. She said because Derek was now moving from side to side and not lying constantly on his back, there was no need for him to wear them. So that was another bonus.

I sat there some time just watching the everyday activities of the ward. Patients were given drugs ready for them to be taken to the operating theatre. It seemed like a ward where patients were only in overnight, had a small operation, and then left the next morning, so there were different faces each day. Some were more sociable than others and would come over to talk to me, as they seemed at a loose end while they waited their turn for the porter to take them to theatre or to be picked up by a family member.

It was late afternoon when Derek stirred and seemed to come wide awake. I asked him if his headache was better, and he started talking. Meanwhile, the nurse came in and said they would sit Derek in the chair for a while. They closed the curtains while I stood by the nurses' desk, as there wasn't very much room near the bed. When they opened the curtains, he was sitting in his chair by the bed next to the window, and he seemed more cheerful.

Stuart had picked the children up from school and drove straight to the hospital, and he asked the nurse if they could see Granddad for a little while. As there were four of them, two went into to see him at a time, which seemed to cheer him up, but again, I was not really sure if he really knew who they were. Stuart stayed for half an hour and then left to get the children back home because they had homework to do, a meal to eat, and then bed, as it was school again tomorrow morning.

My brother, Mick, came to pick me up and said it was the best he had seen Derek looking. Although he still looked very poorly, at least he was awake and talking; sometimes we were not sure what about, but at least it was something.

We tried to think of things to talk about that had happened in the past, the Elvis concerts, past Christmas parties, etc., but I really didn't think he even knew who we were.

As we walked away after the bell rang for the end of visiting time, I turned to wave to him, and he sat with his head slumped, just as though he didn't care about anything. But as my brother had said, we did not know what he was thinking or what was going on inside his head, but surely as each day comes, there must be a slight improvement each time.

I knew Derek did not know where he was, as he hated hospitals and would have crazed to come home if he had known.

CHAPTER 19
Friday, April 6

Gary and Anna were taking me to the hospital today. It was Good Friday, and we knew there would be no outpatients clinic today, so there should be plenty of car-parking spaces.

As soon as we arrived, we could see Derek was looking much better. He had taken a shower, his hair had been washed, and he was clean shaven He had also had the stitches taken out of his hand, although it was still very badly swollen.

Gary said, "What about if we take him downstairs for a wander about. He must get fed up sitting staring at these four walls all day."

So, off I went to find a nurse, and she said no problem and told me to go look for a wheelchair outside one of the other wards. I found one right at the far end of the ward. I asked another nurse if we could have a blanket to cover over Derek. She soon returned with one, and we lifted him in the chair. I knew how to lift him because when my Mum was disabled the community nurse once taught me how to lift someone without hurting your back. Once you got used to it, it was easy to lift even the largest person. The catheter was tucked under the blanket on his lap, and away we went.

Gary pushed the chair along, but it had solid wheels and Derek was finding it was jolting him about. We arrived in the cafeteria and found a table to one side. There weren't many people about and not many food places open, but I could see that one of the counters were displaying a sign for fish and chips. I thought Derek loved them, so off I went to get him some. Gary came with me to help carry them, but the rest of us only wanted chips. Back at the table, I put salt and vinegar on the fish and chips and started to feed Derek. He was just like an infant being fed. Although Derek did not eat much, it was better than nothing.

Gary had finished his chips, and I looked up to say something to Gary and tears were rolling down his cheeks. All of a sudden he jumped up and walked away. I told Anna to go with him, but it wasn't long before the pair of them came back and Gary came with me to get some cups of tea. I asked him what was the matter, and he said he could not bear to see his Dad like that, after knowing how strong and healthy he had been and there I was having to feed him with his meal.

We had seen signs that pointed to the garden so, after we finished our cups of tea, I suggested we walked there to see what it was like. We followed the signs and then went through swing doors out into a lovely little square garden. We followed the brick-weave path under a pagoda. There were garden seats to our right. Turning left, it opened out, still following the brick-weave path, which formed a circle in the middle of it, was a small round garden. The earth was encased in a low brick wall. In the centre was a flowering shrub and then spring flowers around the outside of the shrub.

All the way round the outside was garden that had miniature trees, shrubs, and spring bulbs poking their heads out of the soil. There were a couple of paths that wiggled through the garden, but you always ended up back at the centre. It was really a lovely sun trap. We sat for a little while. Although the sun was shining, it was really chilly, so I took my coat off and wrapped around the front of Derek so there was only his head visible. We decided it was too cold, and we did not want him to catch a cold and make matters worse.

Once back on the ward, I asked him if he wanted to sit in the chair or lay on the bed. He said go on the bed, so I got him in bed and pulled the covers over him, and he went to sleep. Gary and Anna decided to go and left without disturbing him while he was able to sleep.

When he started to rouse, I asked him if he was OK, and he replied, "Oh, I've got a headache."

I went to the nurses' desk to ask if Derek could have a headache tablet. A nurse came in the ward and collected Derek's notes from the rack at the bottom of the bed and recorded what medication she was giving him and what time it was. He swallowed the tablets and then went back to sleep. I got up and went to the toilet and had a little wander about, but when I got back to the bed Derek was then stirring again. I asked how his headache was, and he said it was almost better. Soon after, a nurse came over and told Derek he could sit in the chair for a while, so she helped him into the chair and covered him up with a blanket.

Just after six, the food trolley came round, so I walked into the corridor to see what was on the menu tonight. The staff were all very pleasant, and the man told me the curry is lovely tonight. I explained that Derek only ate very plain English food. I choose some vegetable soup, cottage pie and baked beans, and some rice pudding although it looked very dry, I walked back to the bed and put the food on the table and started to feed Derek with it, but just after a few spoonfuls, he shook his head and said, "No more". Then came the rice, which, after two spoonfuls, again he shook his head and said, "No more".

Then, he looked at me and said, "Take me home."

I wanted to cry, because I would like nothing better to do just that, but I knew it would be a long time yet before that happened.

I said, "Oh love, I would like to take you home, but I can't. You're not well enough yet."

He looked so sad, my heart sank, but on the other hand, I knew he must be improving, otherwise he wouldn't be asking to come home.

Stuart and Caroline arrived, and Derek looked straight at him and said, "Have you come to take me home?"

"Sorry, Dad, I can't," Stuart replied.

I left Stuart and Caroline sitting by the bed while I went to the toilet and then went for a short walk. When I got back, Stuart gave me that look that said Dad was crazing to come home again. Anyway, we kept the conversation going all the time, so Derek had no choice but to sit and listen.

The other patients on the opposite side of the ward had not got any visitors. I suddenly thought if the other patients started talking to Derek and he did not answer them or replied in an unusual manner, they might think him unsociable, so I decided to go over to the man in the bed opposite and explain to him of Derek's injuries and why he might not make conversation with him.

While I was talking to him, apparently Derek said to Stuart, "Why has she gone over to him? Look at her telling him all my business," and kept moaning to Stuart and Caroline about me walking over there.

So, that did not make him very happy. But the man was grateful for me explaining the situation, and said he would talk to him and would understand if he did not get a straightforward reply.

When we left, it wrenched my heart not being able to take him with us.

On the way home, I kept wondering how many hours, days, weeks, or months we were going to have that conversation.

I had trouble trying to get to sleep, because I kept thinking about how long was Derek going to be in hospital and how would we both cope, him wanting to come home and thinking perhaps I did not want him home.

CHAPTER 20
Saturday, April 7

I woke up that morning—it was Easter Saturday—feeling exhausted, as I had tossed and turned all night and just kept waking up thinking what excuses I could keep telling Derek as to why he could not come home. Mike, his mate, was taking me to the hospital, and when he came to pick me up, I explained what we might be faced with today.

But Mike being Mike, he said, "Well, let's just wait and see. He might have forgotten all about it today."

On arrival at the ward, Derek looked very refreshed. He had had a shower and his hair washed, but had not had a shave. I had previously left his electric razor in the locker, so Mike gave him a shave, which made him look even better.

I went along and asked the nurse if we could take him downstairs, We found a wheelchair and pushed him down to the cafeteria. I got us all a cup of tea.

It was very quiet in here today because there were no outpatient clinics, and they did make a big difference. After we sat talking for a little while, I suggested we walk Derek to the gardens, since it was a lovely sunny day and the garden was a sun trap, surrounded by the walls of different hospital departments.

As we walked through the doors and made our way into the garden, there were several members of staff sitting on the benches eating their lunch. Two nurses who had been sitting on a bench in the centre of the garden got up and walked back into the hospital, so we walked over and sat on the bench and manoeuvred the wheelchair at the side of us. We had only been there a few minutes, when a hen blackbird flew down in front of us and started pecking about getting breadcrumbs that the nurses had left. With a beak full, it flew off, but within minutes it was back again and came right up to Derek's chair near his feet. The bird got another beak full and flew off over the low roof of the building to our right.

All of a sudden, Derek said, "That's a hen bird, and she must be feeding some young close by. She'll be back in a minute."

That was the first time he had made a full conversation without being spoken to. Birds and wildlife he loved, and that blackbird must have made an impression on him.

After a while, I could see Derek had had enough, so we slowly pushed him back to the ward and helped him into the chair by the bed. Soon after, Mike left us, and then the dinner trolley came round. To save the staff coming to the bed and telling us what was on the trolley, I always walked out into the corridor and chose something for Derek. I got him some mince, potatoes, and vegetables and a sponge pudding with custard. I started to feed him. He ate a little more today but shook his head and said, "No more." He did not like the sponge pudding, but he ate the custard.

Soon after, the tea trolley came round, and when the lady said, "Tea, coffee, hot chocolate?" Derek asked for tea, which she put in a plastic cup inside a Bakelite holder so as he would not burn himself. Then, she dropped a straw into it. I could see it was hot, so I left it on his locker. Then, all of a sudden, Derek bought the hand that had the splint on it up to his mouth and pursed his lips as though drinking from a cup. I asked him what did he want, and he said he was trying to drink his tea. He obviously thought it was a cup he was holding. This happened three or four times. I went over to his locker and got the drink and held it while he sucked on the straw. After a couple of mouthfuls, he started choking. I rubbed his back, just like you do with a baby. I looked round to see if there was a nurse available, but I was on my own. The coughing gradually lessoned and then stopped—boy, was I relieved!

The bell sounded for visitors to leave until 2.30 p.m. I asked Derek if he would like to get into bed for a little while, and he did, so I helped him onto the side of the bed and lifted his legs in and covered him up. I told him I would be back later and that I was going to get something to eat while he had a sleep.

I made my way to the cafeteria area and sat as usual to eat my lunch and have a mug of tea. I preferred to get my own tea as you could leave the teabag as long as you liked and could also control how much milk you wanted. After I had drunk my tea, I collected all the rubbish and binned it and then walked round the shops as I had another half an hour to spare before visiting time again.

I slowly walked back to the ward, but there were two people standing outside the locked doors to the ward. As you peered through the glass in the doors into the corridor, it was dark because they turned all the light off so the patients could try and go to sleep. The nurse would not open the doors until it was time.

One of the ladies waiting to get in starting moaning and said she had come a long way to visit her husband and could not stay long as she had to get back for the children. She asked how long my husband had been there. Soon, several people arrived. We waited for the doors to open and made conversation with each other, but as soon as the doors were unlocked and everyone went into the different bays in the ward, you perhaps would never see them again.

Derek was fast asleep, so I just sat and watched him. I had taken a puzzle book with me so I sat doing a crossword puzzle, but I just could not seem to concentrate somehow. About four o'clock, Derek's sisters, brother, and brother-in-law came to visit him. I tried to wake Derek by saying, "Come on, look who's come to see you", but he did not stir.

Because of only two visitors to a bed, I said I would go downstairs and leave them there, but Derek's brother, Colin, insisted on coming with me. We walked back to the cafeteria. He gave me the money to go and get a cup of tea for both of us.

Once back at the table, we sat talking about the accident, and Colin admitted he didn't think Derek would have got over the accident the way he had, after seeing him for the first time soon after it happened.

Colin and I chatted about several different things—work, family, grandchildren—and then walked back to the ward, only to find Derek still asleep. The others said he had not moved. They had tried talking to him but got nothing out of him. After they left for home, I sat trying to talk to Derek. The nurse came and checked him over, and I explained we had pushed him to the garden. She thought perhaps it was too much for him, and he was just tired out.

I then heard the familiar sound of the food trolley being pushed along further down the corridor. Derek started to stir, and I began talking to him. He turned and looked at me as much to say, "What you are doing here?"

I wiped his face with a baby wipe and asked if he would like to sit up. I raised the end of the bed and shook his pillows up, and he looked much brighter. I told him he had had visitors but he just said, "Oh!" I asked if he would like something to eat, and he said, "Not really," but I wandered outside to see what was on the trolley—nothing much that Derek liked. I got the plate and put some mashed potato on it and spooned some vegetable soup over it and then put some rice pudding in a bowl and carried back to the bedside. He seemed to enjoy the soup and potato, and then he had a little of the rice. He did not eat it all, but at least he was eating.

Our friends turned up later, and although the conversation was a little one sided, at least he was awake, but you couldn't say he was joining in much. Perhaps he couldn't. Did he know what everyone was talking about?

It was all too soon the bell went off to warn visitors it was time to go. We said our goodnights and left. Dave thought he looked much better than when he had seen him last.

It was a wet journey home, as it had been raining, and there was a lot of spray from the passing cars, but nearer home it left off. On arriving home, we noticed the dog did not run out of the shed to meet us as he always did. Dave drove straight over to where his chain was stretched, and poor old Barney had obviously chased a cat or rabbit round behind the conifer hedge and he had gone round one tree and then back round another one so he was caught up. Dave got out of his car and unclipped the dog. I held on to his collar while Dave unravelled the chain and then clipped him back on. They would not stop for a cup of tea, so I made the wood burner up, took Sally outside, made a cup of tea, and went straight to bed as I felt really tired again tonight.

CHAPTER 21
Easter Sunday, April 8

My niece, Sue, was picking me up that morning, and she was always prompt, so I made sure I fed the dogs and did a few jobs before I went to have a shower and got ready. She is very much like me and would rather be ten minutes early than be five minutes late.

On the way there, she told me as it was Easter Sunday she had bought Derek a basket of small Easter eggs to give him. To him, every day seemed the same. I had just got into that routine of getting up, doing a few jobs, feeding the dogs, and then getting ready to go to the hospital. My thoughts every day were wondering how long Derek would have to be in hospital.

We parked the car, and as we walked through the corridors and neared the stairs to climb to go to the ward, there was a toilet, so I said I must just pop in the loo. She said she had to go too. I came from the toilet and stood in the corridor waiting for Sue. As the door opened and she walked out, I laughed at the sight of her: she had on a headband with pink rabbit ears attached to it. She wore a white blouse and black trousers, and when she turned round, a white fluffy tail was attached to her backside. It was stuck on with Velcro tape. She quickly covered it up by putting on a raincoat and she took out of a carrier bag a small basket of chocolate eggs. As she walked along, the white tail showed through the split seam of her raincoat, and I was giggling. As we walked through the swing doors, she took off her rain coat and walked through the corridor to the end ward, with patients, visitors, and nursing staff all smiling at her.

We walked through the doors to the end bed where Derek was sitting in his chair, and Sue bent over and kissed him. He looked at her, wondering what or who she was. Sue put the basket of eggs on the table and explained why she had brought them. Derek just said, "Thanks."

We sat talking to him for a while, and then I asked the nurse if we could take him downstairs to give him a change of scenery. A short while later, she came back and said it was OK.

I thought how much better he looked today, but he crazed for me to take him home. I tried to explain that I couldn't, but he was just not listening to me. We all enjoyed a coffee. Sue helped me push him back to the ward, and then she left to drive back home.

I fed him his lunch, and then the tea trolley came round and again it was put in a beaker with a straw. His hand was still very swollen but had healed nicely. Because the tea was hot, I left it on the table, but as yesterday, he bought his strapped hand up to his mouth and put his lips together as though he was going to have a drink. I gently pushed his hand down on the bed again and showed him his mug of tea standing on the table. This happened three, perhaps four, times. As soon as his tea was cold enough, I held the mug and fed him with it.

Later, I went and found a wheelchair and told the sister I was going to take Derek for a walk out in the garden. They gave me a blanket to cover over him, and although it was a struggle I managed to get him to the garden with the help of the odd visitor or staff opening doors or helping me in and out of the lift. I found a seat in a sheltered spot and took my mobile phone from my bag and switched it on and dialled Gary's number. After a few words, I gave Derek the phone, and he talked to Gary. Then, shortly afterwards, I rang Stuart so Derek could have a conversation with him as neither boys were coming to the hospital today. I made them take a day off.

After we got back to the ward and I gave him his tea, a couple of friends, Nigel and Diane, arrived. They were part of the Elvis team and were going to take me home that night.

Nigel was holding a large photograph album, which contained several photos of various charity concerts we had performed, so I left them talking and showing Derek the pictures while I went to the cafeteria for a cup of tea and something to eat. While I was sitting there, I realized today was the first time Derek had not fallen asleep in the afternoon, so that was another improvement.

I went back to the ward, and the nurse called me and said they were going to move Derek into Bay D, which was further away from the nurses' desk. When the bell sounded, we got up to leave, and Derek once again asked if he could come home with us. I felt so sorry for him, and he looked so disappointed when I said no. I promised to ask the doctors when they come round in the morning if he could come home. The two nurses were then going to prepare Derek to be moved to Bay D.

On the journey home, Nigel and Diane said he looked better than they had expected but realized he was not interested in the photographs because he did not recognize who the faces were or what the photographs were about.

We chatted on the way home, and once they dropped me off, I let the dog out, made the boiler up, locked the door, made a cup of tea, and went to bed. As I lay there, all sorts of things crept through my mind.

He did not recognize he was Elvis or who anyone else was. Although in some ways there was some improvement, it scared me to think, *Was he going to remember anything about his past? Did he know it was me who sat beside him every day? Did he know it was Gary and Stuart that came to see him? How long would it be before he remembered anything about his past or family or even if he ever would?*

Eventually sleep did come, but not for a long time.

CHAPTER 22
Easter Monday, April 9

Gary was taking me to the hospital this morning; Anna was unable to come as she was working at the hotel today.

Keith arrived just before we were about to leave and said that Derek had rung them about nine the night before and his wife, Joan, had answered the call. Derek asked her what our fax number was, as he needed it because he was stuck in his truck on the M25. Keith said it had upset Joan because it did not seem like the usual Derek at all. I was just as puzzled as Keith and began to worry that, being in a confused state of mind, would he attempt to ring someone else tonight.

It was not a bad journey considering it was a holiday weekend.

Derek was still on A3 ward, but had been moved from the room behind the nurses' desk to further along the corridor.

We arrived at the new bay where Derek had been moved to. His bed was on the left-hand side as you walked in the bay, but instead of being close to the window, he was in the middle bed. Still nothing much could be seen from the window. The rooftop outside was perhaps slightly lower than the previous ward. The man who was in the end bed at the window had obviously had a brain operation and was propped up on pillows but was fast asleep. There was a young man in the bed just inside the door. He was sitting up, talking to a young girl and a couple I assumed were his parents, but they were not speaking English. There were three beds on the opposite side occupied by men who had all had operations on their heads.

It amazed me that we never ever got a smile from Derek when we went in the ward. He just said his usual hello, and we kept chatting to him. Then, all of a sudden, he started talking about Tony Blair and dropping a bag of fertilizer from Gary's truck onto him and saying loads of numbers. We were certainly puzzled over this. Had he been dreaming? But he kept on about the same thing all the time we were there. The only thing I could think of was that he liked to watch war documentaries. Gary and he had hauled fertilizer, and Tony Blair was prime minister. His mind was confused, and he had gotten the three things mixed up. Instead of bombs dropping from the plane, it was bags of fertilizer.

When I tried to explain to him that Gary's truck could not fly, he said, "Yes, it can. The doors open underneath, and you can drop it out." (Gary's truck was an articulated curtain side with doors that opened at the back.)

Gary could see a huge improvement in Derek since he had seen him on Friday. Once again we walked downstairs had a cup of drink and then walked him to the garden. There were several people sitting out there. The slight breeze was very cool, so we decided not to stay to long and walked him back to the ward.

Gary sat telling Derek of all the people that had rang him, asking after him and what work he had been doing. Then, the question came up, "Are you going to take me home with you?"

I had promised I would ask a doctor today, but as it was Easter Monday there were no doctors' rounds just a ward doctor on duty in case he was needed. I had to try and explain there was no one present to give their consent today, but he still kept on. We tried changing the subject, but it always ended up the same thing: "Get me out of here. I want to go home."

The lunch trolley came round, and I got him some tomato soup, shepherd's pie and some kind of sponge pudding. He ate the soup and some of the pie, and after a couple of spoonfuls of the pudding, he shook his head, much as to say "No more". Then, the trolley with the drinks arrived, and he had a cup of tea. At home he would never touch tea; he only ever drank coffee. I could see that he did not enjoy his meal at all.

Gary stayed until the visitor's bell sounded at one o'clock, and we left, so Derek could have a sleep. I told him I would be back shortly, as I was going to have a cup of tea.

So, Gary and I got a drink, a burger and chips each, and sat for an hour chatting, catching up on other events as I had been so engrossed in hospital life for so long.

Just before it was time to go back to the ward, I walked back to the car with Gary to get some fresh air and watched him drive off. I walked slowly back to the ward but the doors were still locked and other visitors were waiting outside, so we were making polite conversation about who we had come to visit and how long a journey we had all had to get there and of course the car parking charges. I explained that you could buy a £20 parking ticket that lasted for fourteen days and would work out much cheaper than paying on a daily basis, but some explained that they only came every other day, others only stopped an hour, and some only made a special journey to see a friend or distant relative. So, it looked as though I was the only one from about six people waiting to visit on this ward who came in daily and stopped all day, although I was not driving there. The family brought me and used the parking ticket between them.

I walked in the ward and asked Derek if he had been a sleep and he shook his head no. I had noticed that the young man's family had remained on the ward, while other visitors had to leave. The man in the next bed was still asleep. I tried to make conversation with Derek, but all he kept on about was dropping fertilizer on Tony Blair from a great height. I began to wish I had not taken that war documentary in the high-dependency ward for him to look at, as there were planes flying over enemy territory dropping bombs that had definitely confused him. I kept talking about the grandchildren and the dogs, but he never made any comments about them at all.

He just kept saying, "I want to get out of here", which concerned me, because at some stage I would have to bring some clothes in for him. Would he just walk out of hospital and get lost? I then plucked up courage to ask why he had telephoned Keith and Joan for our fax number and his reply was that he had tried ringing me and I was out, so he called them. I explained that we were still travelling on the way home from seeing him, and he had not given us time to get home

Derek kept trying to get comfortable in his chair. Although he was sitting on a pillow, he could not get comfortable. A nurse came into the room and asked Derek if he was OK. He said, "Yes, thank you," but I told the nurse he could not sit very comfortable. He had kept saying his bottom hurt, so she said she would find him a better chair to sit in. About twenty minutes later, she came back with an arm chair like you have in the lounge at home, but this had larger wheels on it so it was easy to push about. We could push him to the garden or cafeteria in it. I helped her to swap the chairs over, and she settled Derek back into it and he said that felt better. It was more comfortable than the other one he had sat in, as that was more of an upright solid, chair with a leather cushion and wooden arms.

Soon after, the food trolley approached, and as usual I went out into the corridor to see what there was today. I decided to get him cottage pie and baked beans and some rice pudding. I took it back to the bed side and started to feed him. He had almost eaten the cottage pie but then shook his head that he did not want anymore. He did not go a bundle on the rice pudding either, but I told him if he did not eat, the longer he would be in hospital, because he had to get his strength back in his legs to walk.

Stuart and Caroline appeared through the doors, and I sat talking to them for a while and then said I was going for a cup of tea. It was so hot in the ward that it made me feel dry, as well as tired.

I wondered off and went to the self-service counter and got a drink, selected a muffin and a tub of fresh fruit salad, and sat at a table. As it was Easter Monday, very few visitors where in the cafeteria. Once I had finished, I made my way slowly back to the ward.

Conversation was very hard, even with Caroline and Stuart there, as all Derek was interested in was to get out of the hospital. All too soon, we had to leave him once again. It was getting more difficult for me, as I knew what he must be going through.

He could not have a conversation with the men either side of him, however small it might have been. The older man slept all the time and did not even wake up when his wife came to see him. The young man on the other side could not speak English. The men opposite kept themselves amused by watching television or reading.

We said our goodbyes, and once again I promised Derek I would see if the doctor would let him come home tomorrow, but I knew in my heart that would not be possible until he had regained his strength.

Stuart and Caroline did not know about Derek ringing Keith until I told them on the way home, and they too became concerned as we all tried to come up with answers as to why he needed the fax number and tried to fathom out why he thought he was on the M25. He must have thought he was delivering one of his loads or going to make a collection. Until something happens like this, you do not realize how one's mind really works. I lay in bed thinking what tomorrow would bring and hoping that Derek did not ring anyone tonight.

CHAPTER 23

Tuesday, April 10

Every morning when I woke, the very first thing that came into my head was that the hospital had not called me in the night.

I did the usual chores and fed dogs and got myself ready for another day. My sister, June, and her husband, John, came to collect me.

Although making conversation in the car on the way to Cambridge, my mind kept going back as to whether there would be any further improvement in Derek today.

When we arrived at the bedside, he seemed cheerful and was talking to us, and then all of a sudden, the conversation veered round to dropping on Tony Blair from a great height. He just kept on and on about it. Whatever else we might discuss, trying to change the subject, Derek turned it back to trucks in the sky, Tony Blair, and dropping fertilizer from great heights. We all kept thinking of things to talk about that would interest Derek. Sometimes we got him to join in, and I would think, *At last he has forgot about Tony Blair,* and then the sound of an aeroplane overhead would start it all up again.

The doctor came round and stood by the bedside and said that Derek was doing really well. I asked if Derek could come home because he was only sitting in the chair all day, which he

The Three Birds

could do at home, and the doctor just shook his head from side to side and shouted, "No!"

I looked at Derek and said, "I did promise to ask the doctor. Now will you believe me that you cannot come home?" and he looked like a little boy who had been naughty.

The doctor looked at Derek's very swollen hand and said the cast must come off and he must have some physiotherapy exercises to reduce the swelling. About twenty minutes later, the physiotherapy nurse came to the bed and said could I meet her by the bed at one thirty.

As usual, the food trolley could be heard coming along the corridor, so I left the bed and went to see what was on the menu today. Again, there were a lot of things Derek did not like, but I got some potato and stewed meat and some jam sponge pudding. I walked back to the bed and started feeding him. After a few spoonfuls, he shook his head, and said, "No more". He only ate a very small piece of the sponge pudding and custard. Then, the lady came with the tea trolley, and Derek once again asked for a cup of tea. The nurse passed over the beaker of tea to me with a straw in it, and we left it to cool before Derek could drink it. It was strange because he would still bring the hand that was in the cast and try and make a fist shape as though he was holding the cup and bring it up to his mouth and then purse his lips as though trying to drink from it.

I would say, "No, Derek, your drink is on your table waiting to cool down," and then I would hold the beaker for him to drink from but as always as soon as he had some tea he would start coughing.

The nurse kept a record of everything Derek ate and drank each day, and today when the nurse emptied his catheter bag and came back shortly afterwards, she told Derek he must drink more fluids. I explained he did not drink much during the day before his accident anyway, but she said he must try.

I walked with June and John back to the restaurant area. From there on, they knew where to walk to the car. June asked whatever was that all about that Derek kept saying about Tony

Blair, and I had to explain that when the doctor had come to see Derek to test what state his mind was in, the doctor would ask Derek who is the prime minister, what year is it, what hospital are you in. The only thing he got right was Tony Blair.

I headed back for the ward and sat by the bed. The visitors' bell had gone, and apart from myself, the only other people left on the ward were the young lad's parents just inside the door, when in came the ward manager.

She looked straight at me and said, "Did you not hear the bell for visitors to leave?"

I explained that the physiotherapist had asked me to meet her by the bed at 1.30 p.m.

She said, "Well, you can't wait in here, this is time for the patients to have a sleep. You will have to go sit in the day room until it's time for you to meet the physiotherapist."

Which is I what did, but I noticed she never told the other visitors to leave.

So, I watched the clock very slowly tick by until it was time to go as instructed to wait by the bed. I had just got in the ward, when the young physio appeared.

It was obvious that the doctor had spoken to her, because she went on to say that I had asked if Derek could go home and she explained the reason why it would be too difficult for me to manage Derek at home.

She then went on to help Derek from his bed, stood him up, and then said we were going to walk into the long corridor that ran alongside each bay. So, with his handbag (catheter) we got into the corridor, and she asked me to walk on Derek's right side. With the aid of the physio we all started to walk forward, but every two or three steps Derek would start to fall to his right, which was the side I was standing. We only walked from his bay to the next one and then turned round and started back.

The physio said, "That's why he cannot go home yet. He has a weakness on his right side that we must try and get strengthened up. So, it will mean several visits to the gym."

By the time Derek got back to the bed, he had had enough, and like a child got into bed, and I tucked him up. The physio said she would send a porter for him the next afternoon, and I could go to the gym with him.

After she had walked away, Derek said, "I'm not going to any bloody gym."

I replied, "You will be in hospital a lot longer if you don't. They are only trying to build up your muscles in your legs, and so until you can walk on your own, you will stay here."

Derek seemed tired, so I said I would have to leave as it still was not visiting time as yet, and I would go for my lunch, while he had a sleep.

On my return to the ward, I saw the nursing manager on the steps leading up to A3 ward, so I stopped and ask her why I was made to leave and the other visitors were left on the ward. She spoke very abruptly and said that she had no reason to explain to me the situation of that patient, but it had to do with the language barrier. She then left and continued in the opposite direction.

I got back to the bedside, and the first words Derek said to me were "Can I come home?"

I asked if he had really listened to what the physio had said, and he shrugged his shoulders and then went very quiet. I told him that I would willingly love to have him home to look after him, but if the medical team says no, then I cannot go against them. It was a very long afternoon for me, as Derek seem as though he went into a sulk and eventually he fell asleep.

The wife came to visit her husband in the bed next to the window, but he did not stir either, so we made conversation and exchanged why our husbands were in hospital, but after an hour, she said she might as well leave as it looked as though her husband wasn't going to wake and with that she left, as she had an hour's journey to get home.

Soon after, the tea trolley arrived, and I got Derek his usual beaker of tea but decided to let him sleep. As the nurse pushed the tea trolley back along the corridor, the clattering along made Derek wake up. He sat up, and I helped him drink his afternoon cuppa.

Derek told me that he had a headache once again; perhaps he had slept too soundly. So, when the nurse came into the ward, I asked if Derek could have some pain relief, which she said she would go and get him something. Soon after, she was back with some tablets, which he swallowed, and then he lay back down with his eyes closed.

Later, I asked Derek if he fancied some chips for his tea, but when the trolley came round there did not seem anything on there he wanted. He said, "If you like", so I went to the cafeteria and asked them for some chips to take away, which they put in a polystyrene box. Then, I went to the self-service counter and bought some sachets of salt and vinegar.

Back on the ward, the nurses said, "Oh, I can smell chips."

I asked if they minded if I gave them to Derek, and they said it was no problem. He had started to feed himself with the chips, as there was no knife or fork involved, but he did not eat them all, so I helped myself to the rest.

I remembered the food trolley was still parked outside the next bay along the corridor and went to see what dessert they had left, and I decided to take some fruit crumble and custard back for him. He tried to feed himself, but he could not hold the spoon in his right hand, so he had a go at holding it in his left hand and began to feed himself. However, the custard was dribbling down the corners of his mouth, and he was dropping spoonfuls of it in his lap, so I had to take over and help feed him. By this time, he said his headache was a little better.

Derek's mate was coming to pick me up but would not have time to come to the ward during visitor's hour as he worked until 6.00 p.m. Then had to get home, have his tea, and then it was an hour's journey, depending on the traffic, so I arranged to meet him in the car park just after 8.00 p.m.

The nurse came in to ask Derek how his headache was, and said he had still got one, so she said, "I will leave the lights off in the room for now and that might help you."

It seemed as though it was getting really dusk in the room. Then, in came another nurse and said, "What's all this? No lights on in here?"

I explained that the other nurse had left the lights off because of Derek's headache. She just smiled and went out of the room.

All too soon it was time to say goodnight, and I told him that I would be back in the morning, kissed him, and left.

I felt really tired that night, so after seeing to the dogs, I made myself a cup of drink and went to bed. I had just got into bed when the telephone rang. I looked at the clock and it was 10.30 p.m. On this telephone by the bed I did not have a caller display. I was a bit dubious about answering that time of night, but thought it might be one of the boys.

I picked up the receiver and said, "Hello."

A weak voice on the other end said, "Hello, it's only me. Where have you been? I tried to ring you before, but you were out."

I replied, "Oh, Derek, what's the matter? I've come straight home from the hospital, seen to the dogs and the boiler, had a shower, and I'm now in bed."

He said, "Can you ring this farmer?" and then went on to give me a mobile number.

He repeated the number again and said, "Now make sure you ring him."

He never gave any reason why or what I should tell the farmer. I had no intentions of calling anyone, but he still kept insisting that I get the number down. I told him I would call the farmer as soon as I put the phone down. I told him I would see him tomorrow, and with that he seemed satisfied and just said "Good night" and was gone.

Sleep would not come, as I had visions of Derek ringing other people up and what would their reaction be.

I decided I would go and see the duty nurse as soon as I got to the ward and talk to her about Derek making these calls.

CHAPTER 24
Wednesday, April 11

My niece, Sue, drove into the yard to take me to the hospital. She had been to collect my two sisters, Joyce, and of course her mum, Sylv. I joined them and we chatted along the way. Joyce remarked that she could not make the journey every day to Cambridge, it must be so tiring.

Sylv walked with me to the bay where Derek was.

He seemed in a better mood today, and then I looked and said, "Oh you've had your catheter removed. That's good."

I asked the nurse if we could take Derek to the cafeteria, and the nurse said it was no problem. We could push him in the chair he already sat in. I went to the desk and asked for a blanket. Once Derek was covered with the blanket, we made our way to the lift. It was a large chair to try and steer straight, but we made our way to join the others.

I pushed the chair toward Joyce and Sue, when Sue started to raise her voice saying, "Chris, Chris, you're running over the water bag."

Puzzled at what she was talking about, I looked down and there was the catheter bag. I know my mouth fell open, and when I looked again the nurse had put the tube down the inside leg of Derek's pyjama leg and the catheter bag had just lain on the floor behind the foot plate of the chair, out of sight. I felt embarrassed as to what would have happened if I had run over the bag and it had burst.

Visitors were looking and smiling as I hauled the bag from the floor and desperately tried to conceal it. It just reached the seat of the chair beside Derek, and I quickly covered it with the blanket.

At least we had made Derek smile, and it was a standing joke for a while. Sue walked over to one of the coffee bars and came back with a tray of hot drinks, she said, "I got Derek a cup of latte for a change", but it was far too hot for him to drink. I picked up a teaspoon and kept giving him spoonfuls of what looked very much like drinking chocolate. When there was half a cup left, he shook his head, no more.

Derek seemed more alert today and did not waffle on like he had the previous days; he was not a great conversation maker, but at least he answered their questions

After an hour, he began to hang his head as though he had not got the strength to hold it up anymore, so I said I would push him back to the ward. Sue walked with me, and we got him back to the ward. I said once he had had something to eat, he could lie on the bed for a sleep before he went to the gym. Sue and my sisters left for home, and I would stay with him until the visitors' bell sounded.

I fed him some dinner, which he did not enjoy, and when the tea trolley came round he shook his head, as he did not want anything to drink

I had taken him a bottle of squash and asked if he would like a cold drink, but he said no. He never did drink very much during the day, even during the summer months. Years ago, when he was working out in the harvest fields, a bottle of diluted squash would last him two or three days. He could never drink a pint of beer. To him, as he had said, if you had a large meal and then someone puts another in front of you, you can't eat it because you are full and that's what a glass of beer felt like to him. Just then the bell sounded, so I helped him into bed for a sleep and left, but instead of turning left to go out of the ward, I turned right to go to the nurse's desk.

Coming out of one of the bays a male nurse almost bumped into me, and he asked, "Did you get your phone call OK last night?"

I looked puzzled but said yes.

The nurse said, "After you had left, Derek had crazed and crazed to call you to give you a mobile number. In the end he got so frustrated I had to let him use my mobile."

I then explained that was why I was heading for the nurse's desk, so we walked to the desk together. I told him and another nurse that, if Derek ever wanted to ring anyone, whoever it might be, they should dial my number for Derek. I explained how he had rang Keith's number and it had upset his wife. They made a note of this and said no problem. What a relief that was sorted out.

I went and sat in the cafeteria to eat my usual salad and cup of tea. I looked at the time, and it just seemed to drag. Until it was time to go back to the ward, I wondered around the few shops that were situated just through the main entrance hall. You had to walk by the shops to get to the wards or in the opposite direction to the cafeteria.

The shops included a florist that also did a roaring trade in helium balloons with different messages on them, two mini markets, one selling newspapers, cold drinks, sandwiches and cakes, and the other one catering more for the patient, anything from toiletries and reading books to a small selection of slippers and pyjamas, as well as confectionary, a ladies' clothes shop, a hairdressers, and the last one was a small gift shop.

As you walked in from the car-park entrance at the rear of the hospital, you came along a corridor and turned left for the food hall or right to go by the shops, wards, and clinics. As you turned right from the corridor, there used to be a section where a market trader or shop owner, I guess, would come into the hospital and set the goods on display to sell. There would be a different trader there each day. One day, there would be a large selection of handbags and purses. Another day would be jewellery, then towels and bed linen. I also saw pictures for sale and different sizes and colours of picture frames, and one day a huge selection of shoes, some with heels "that high". I wondered how anyone could possibly walk in them, but the owner of the products would sit quietly on a chair at the end of their display reading or chatting to would-be customers. There was never any pressure to buy anything. You could just browse.

I made my way back to the ward and only had to wait a few minutes before the visitors were let in. When I got back to Derek, he was sitting in his chair. He said he had been asleep, and the nurse had just put him in the chair. There was no way at this moment in time he could stand on his own. Sometimes, I would have to fight back the tears when watching him trying to achieve what was such a simple task to me, but it was sometimes impossible for him to do.

I thought how much better he looked for the sleep he had. He even asked me where Sue and my sisters were, and I explained they left ages ago. At that moment, a porter came in pushing a wheelchair and asked for Mr Russell, saying, "I've come to take you to the gym."

We approached double doors on the left hand side, which was clearly marked "GYM," and the double doors in front of us led to the garden. The porter pushed the chair through the doors and parked it up in gym.

There were a couple of patients doing different exercises helped by young physiotherapists. It made me feel quite old, looking at these young girls and thinking they only looked like school girls, but I suppose I am getting up the tooth a bit.

The room reminded me of the gym we had at school (yes—I have got a good memory) except we never had any beds in the gym at our school. Baskets of rubber balls stood in one corner with sets of wooden stairs with four or five steps to climb, different exercise machines, treadmill, climbing frames at the side of the wall, and various other equipment.

The doors behind us opened again, and another porter parked another patient in a wheelchair behind the one Derek was sitting in. Then, the young lady came in that was to give Derek his exercises.

She managed to get Derek out of the chair and asked me to walk on his right side and she walked on his left. We walked very slowly to the middle of the room and then slowly turned in the direction toward the bed and laid him on it, and she started to do various exercises with his legs—then, back on his feet again.

The physio said, "It's a lovely day outside. Let's walk to the garden."

Again, one each side of Derek, we walked out into the sunshine. I could see that the bright light was making him squint, but that was only natural being in the ward all day.

He was doing really well, still tending to fall to the right but not as often as he did yesterday in the corridor. We walked back and sat him in his wheelchair, ready to go back to the ward. I told the young lady that I could push Derek back to the ward, but she said the porter was on his way with another patient and he would take Derek back.

When we got back to the ward, he sat in his chair, and I asked what he thought of the gym.

He replied, "Not bad, but wait until I have to go on all them machines in there."

All too soon the food trolley came rattling along and stopped outside the bay. I went to investigate what was on the menu tonight and reported back to Derek. I asked him if he would like me to go and get some chips from downstairs. He replied that he got fed up with chips. I remember it was curry or pasta on that night, which Derek did not like, so off to the cafeteria. I came back with shepherd's pie and baked beans, which he tried to feed himself with a spoon but was making a mess, so I helped him and then went to the food trolley along the corridor to get him a dessert—fruit crumble and custard.

Soon after, Gary came, and I left him to talk to his dad while I went for a walk and something to eat.

On the way home, Gary said he could not believe how well Dad was getting on.

He said, "He has a long way to go, but he looks better than he did the week before."

As we were driving along, ahead of us we noticed a fluorescent board "POLICE ACCIDENT" then another one said "DIVERSION" with the arrow pointing to our left. It was really ironic, as we turned left and followed some other cars that had also taken this small narrow road. Gary said he hadn't a clue where we are going to. Then, we turned right at another junction, following the car in front through a small village, when Gary realized he had delivered to a farm just along the road from where we were but had entered the farm from a different direction, twisting and turning. The number of cars we were meeting dazzled me with their lights. We finally reached the Ely roundabout, where boards stood closing the road to our right on the A10. We turned left onto the A10 and made our way home.

I said to Gary, "Blimey, it's a good job you were driving as I would not have a clue where to go."

I had noticed during the day that Derek had started swearing in nearly every sentence he made, and Gary had also noticed this during his visit and made a comment about it as well.

I took a cup of tea to bed and thought through the day's events and felt very proud of Derek today as I knew he is trying very hard. It was so very sad that such an active man could be reduced to being almost helpless within a few hours.

CHAPTER 25

Thursday, April 12

I wondered what the day would bring. I thought that if I could possibly be travelling back and forth to Cambridge for several weeks to come, then I would soon suggest starting driving myself there, as I could not keep relying on family and friends to take me when I knew Derek was out of danger.

One of our friends, David, who Derek had known from school days, was taking me to the hospital this morning, and on the way I bought him up to date with all that had happened over the past week, although he was in constant contact with Gary to see what progress Derek was making.

On our arrival, Derek was sitting in the chair by the bed. I thought perhaps David coming to see him would cheer him up a little, but the expression on his face never really changed. Although he sat talking to David, I began to wonder if Derek knew who he was talking to.

I left David chatting to Derek while I went for a walk, as I thought it would make a change for Derek to have someone completely different to talk to. I would be with Derek the rest of the day.

I went to have a cup of tea and then walked to have a look round the shop to see if there was something different I could get Derek to eat. I got some crisps, muffins, sweets, and some chocolate. After all, he had to put that three stone back on.

I arrived back to the ward and tried to tempt Derek with something to eat from the goodies I had bought from the shop, but he did not want anything, not even a sweet.

The meal trolley arrived, and Derek said he did not want anything to eat and I began to wonder if he was feeling poorly. I asked him what he had had for breakfast, but he could not remember.

I did get him some food, but he just picked it about. He did eat the dessert, and then I encouraged him to eat one of the blueberry muffins and I helped him with his cup of tea.

When the visitors' bell went, I asked David if he would like something to eat before he left. He replied no, but I told him to come on since I was going to have something. We sat with a sandwich and a cup of tea, and he left me just before it was time to go back to the ward.

As I walked back through into the bay for the afternoon visiting, I saw Derek holding the remote control that should be used to alter the position of the bed by raising or lowering either end and adjusting the centre.

He looked at me, waving the remote about, and said, "Where have you been? I have been trying to ring you but can't get through."

I said, "Derek, that is not a mobile phone. It's the remote to control your bed."

"No it isn't," he replied, "it's a phone."

I think I must have tried to explain four or five times that it was not a phone and even took the remote and made the bed go up and down, but he still insisted it was a mobile. How could I convince him? Can you imagine what the other patients thought, to see Derek's bed being lowered and raised at each end as Derek pressed the remote buttons—something only Mr Bean would do.

A tall, well-dressed gentleman walked up to the bed and said, "Hello, Derek. How are you?"

Derek looked as puzzled as I was until the gentleman, named Ian, explained that he was the director from a company that in the previous years had arranged haulage work with Derek. I had never met him, but had heard Derek talk of him.

I explained how Derek was getting confused trying to ring me on the remote for the bed, and Ian was able to change the subject for a while. We could hear small aircraft overhead flying in or out of Cambridge airport, and that seem to upset Derek again, as he started to ramble on about the same old story of Tony Blair dropping fertilizer out of Gary's trailer up in the sky.

Ian left after about an hour, and I walked as far as the lift with him and explained how Derek got confused. He said it must be hard for me to have to sit and listen to Derek getting confused and be unable to help him. But, as I said, it could have been a lot worse—he could have been paralyzed for life.

Derek asked me if he could come home, and I said we would have to ask the doctor, which I did, when the surgeon came along with some trainee doctors. He asked Derek what year it was, and Derek replied, "1972". Then, the doctor asked what hospital was he in. Derek thought for a moment and then replied, "Cambridge eye hospital."

The surgeon looked straight at me and said, "No, he can't go home, but we will transfer him to King's Lynn hospital when there is a bed available" And he walked out of the ward.

Soon after, a porter arrived to take Derek to the gym, so off we went. Derek walked round the inside of the gym with the aid of the physio and then had to lie on the bed and was shown various exercises he could do on the bed in the ward, but nothing very energetic today.

He did not eat very much at all today. Derek said he was not hungry.

Derek's mate came to pick me up tonight, and once he had arrived, as usual, I went to get a cup of drink and something to eat and left those two to chat.

I sat at the table drinking my tea and just kept thinking, *Where is this all going to end?* Every day the conversation included this question: "When can I come home?" And every time I would say that, I would ask the doctor.

Twice today Derek had said, "Oh, it's you that don't want me to come home. You would rather me stay here."

It was very hurtful, as I would like nothing better for him to be at home, but he did not understand the situation.

On the ward, Mike sat looking at a book on old tractors that I had taken for Derek to look at. Mike was asking Derek all sorts of questions about each model, so I just sat back and listened. Again, Derek was swearing a lot, and I had to keep saying, "Shush, Derek, the other patients will hear you."

Stuart and Caroline said they might come to see Derek because they were both back at work, and Stuart's shift pattern meant he could not always make the visitors' times. I looked at my watch, and it was almost eight o'clock. I thought they would not be coming as the bell sounded. I had taken some sunglasses for Derek to wear to protect his eyes from the bright day light and the ward lights at night. There Derek sat looking like Roy Orbison.

I stood in the corridor waiting for Mike to finish talking to Derek. When I looked up, Stuart and Caroline came through the doors and along the corridor. I asked one of the nurses if it would be OK for them to see Derek for five minutes and explained Stuart had come straight from work. The nurse said it would be fine, so Mike wandered off and waited in the corridor near the exit doors.

After nearly ten minutes, Stuart and Caroline said they had better make a move so the three of us said our good nights and Derek said, "Are you going to take me home with you?"

Stuart said, "Oh, Dad, I can't."

We made our way through the open doors of his bay into the corridor and turned to wave at him. There Derek sat with his sunglasses on. He looked straight at Stuart and said, "W★★★a," and then he stared straight ahead to the wall opposite his bed and never looked back at us.

Of course, Stuart made the biggest laugh out of what his Dad had called him and still to this day he often reminds his Dad of what had been said.

We all made our way to the car park, and I went home with Mike because Stuart and Caroline could then go straight home along the A10 instead of going through all the back roads to take me home. Since Mike lived at the other end of the village, it was not out of his way.

As Mike drove along he started to laugh and said, "What do you think? I was sitting looking at that tractor book, and Derek was talking away. I knew some of the things I was talking about, but Derek did not know who I was. So I said, 'You don't know who I am, do you?' and he replies, 'No, but who effing cares. It's someone to talk to.'"

CHAPTER 26
Friday, April 13

It was Friday the thirteenth. Sylv had called in to see me as usual, and she mentioned the date almost as soon as she came in the door as she is very superstitious. It's funny really, as she was born on the thirteenth, but I never would let Friday the thirteenth bother me.

Many years ago, while on holiday in Scotland, we were browsing around in a shop and saw the crest badge of the name Russell in the shape of a shield covered with the Russell tartan and in the centre was a ram with the Scottish thistle in its mouth. The words inscribed on the front as the Russell motto were "Che Sarà, Sarà", which translated is "Whatever will be, will be", so we got it and put it up on the wall.

After the usual chat, she left so I could get ready for the day ahead.

June and John picked me up and we made our way to Cambridge. We walked into the bay and saw Derek looking considerably brighter and chatting away with us, which was most unusual.

We decided to take him to the cafeteria for a change of scenery, I just wish he could get rid of that catheter, as you had to make sure the tube was not twisted when I laid it on his lap and I wheeled him about, but I suppose that cannot come out until he can walk on his own to the toilet. I pushed him in his wheelchair, and we all headed for the garden area and then all went to the cafeteria.

We heard nothing about Tony Blair or trucks flying in the air.

I got him some chips, but he never ate them all. I think he was totally bored with the food I kept choosing for him. I just wished there was some way I could bring some home-cooked food in, but that would be a problem to keep it hot from when I left home to lunch time.

When it was time, I wheeled him back to the ward for his afternoon nap while June and John waited for me to return to the cafeteria. I then walked back to the car with them because she had made me my favourite egg sandwiches and a yogurt. We sat in the car, and I really enjoyed the sandwiches.

Back on the ward, Derek was still on his bed, but said he had not been asleep, so I helped him into the chair and we sat talking. I had told the physio that I would push Derek to the gym at three o'clock this afternoon as the porters had enough to do. Near the time, I went and found a wheelchair, and we made our way to the gym. There were only a couple of patients there. After a couple of minutes, Derek's physio came in and straight away walked Derek to one side of the room, got a ball, threw it to me, and asked me to stand opposite Derek. I was to gently throw the ball to him, to see how his reflexes were. I threw the ball several times. The first time it rolled to the right. The second time it rolled to the left, and this went on and on. I was knackered as it was me that had to keep running from one side to the other to retrieve the ball.

I could have done with a lay down myself after that. Well, it was the first exercise I had had since Derek had been in Addenbrookes, because I was sitting down most of the time.

The physio made Derek walk up and down the small wooden staircase three times. The first time, he was very wobbly, but after then, he did really well. Then, he had to lie on the bed and do some exercises to strengthen the muscles in his legs. And then, to my surprise, she said that she was going to walk Derek back to the ward. By that, she meant not in a wheelchair. She held on to his arm and took a different route to the way I knew. It seemed as though we just kept walking, and then, we stopped in front of the lift. We waited for the doors to open and stepped in. We were only in there a few seconds, and when the doors opened we stepped out right outside the ward doors.

He said he felt OK, just that his legs ached, which is understandably as it was the first time he had used his legs.

Derek sat in the chair but seemed very quiet. I asked him what was wrong. He replied, "Nothing", but I noticed he kept putting his hand on his tummy, and I again asked if he had a bellyache. He said yes, so I suggested, that I would walk him to the toilet. At first, he refused, but then he said, "OK." As I opened the door, a lady was sitting on the toilet.

"Oops, sorry," I said and closed the door quick.

We then walked back past the ward and found another toilet to use, but it was a false alarm. We sat talking, and he said he wanted to go back to the toilet, so off we walked again.

On the third occasion, the ward doctor was walking by, and he turned round and said, "Well done. It's good to see you mobile."

I felt more confident now walking with Derek as he did not seem as wobbly; I suppose he was getting the strength back in his legs. Also, he was less confused today—another small improvement.

The physio had given him some exercises to do to get the swelling down on his hand. Some friends appeared through the door. They were staying a few miles from the hospital on a camp site. Once they had found a chair, they gave Derek a small, soft ball, which Derek could squeeze in his hand to try and help exercise it. He kept dropping it on the floor, but with practice I was sure he would get the hang of it.

He had missed his afternoon cup of tea, and I would have gone back down to get him a cup of hot chocolate but he said not to bother.

A nurse came in and called to Derek, "You've missed your cup of tea. I'll go and make you one."

Only a few minutes later, she returned with the beaker of tea and stood it on his table to cool down.

When the tea trolley arrived, the friends left, and I went to see what Derek could eat tonight. He's such a fussy eater. He likes all his food to be plain and simple, with no spices or sauces. The only thing he liked was once again shepherd's pie and beans. I took the plate back to the bedside table and then went back to get a dessert. I always served up Derek's food myself. The man who pushed the trolley and served meals would always get outside our bay and then start singing one of Elvis Presley's songs. He was always busy attending to the other patients, and the first time I stood at the trolley and asked for something, he said, "Oh, just come out and serve yourself," so I always did.

I got some sponge pudding with custard, as I knew Derek would like that, but I could see by his face, he never really enjoyed what he was eating. He would eat so much and then shake his head, no more.

Friends, Dave and Sylvie, who lived in the same village were coming to visit Derek that night and then take me home, so once they had arrived, I left to get something to eat. If it was nice weather, I would walk outside for some fresh air and then go back to the ward.

As we were leaving, I bent down and kissed Derek and said, "See you tomorrow" and he looked at me and said, "Please take me home."

I said, "A few more days and perhaps I can, Love."

I always felt awful walking away and leaving him. Usually, Derek would talk to anyone, but he just seemed to sit staring ahead.

On the way home, I said I wished there was some way I could cook some food and take for Derek, but there was no way I could keep it hot. I explained although the food trolley came round with a selection of hot food twice a day, at lunch and evening times, I was not sure how the breakfast was served because I was never there and Derek could never remember what he had eaten for breakfast. Derek never seemed to enjoy his food.

Dave said, "I'm sure we have got a soup flask somewhere. If we can find it, I'll drop it into you."

Today had been a good day for Derek, and I was really pleased that he had started walking around the ward.

CHAPTER 27
Saturday, April 14

I was already for Gary and Anna to arrive this morning when there was a knock on the door. It opened and a familiar voice called, "Are you about?"

It was Dave. He had the soup flask in his hand. It was a red container with a beige-coloured screw lid. It was not very tall but larger in the circumference than a normal flask. I told him that would be brilliant. Just then, Gary arrived. After a few minutes, Dave left and so did we.

One of the nurses had said they like the patients to get dressed if possible, and I had kept saying I was going to take Derek some clothes to wear as everyone else on the ward was dressed, except of course those who were still not able to get out of bed. So, Stuart was going to get some jogging bottoms for him today as we thought that would be easier for him to pull on and off.

As soon as we had arrived on the ward Gary said, "Let's take dad to the cafeteria. It will make a change from staring at these four walls."

Off Gary went to find a wheelchair as he said the one Dad was sitting in was too big to push and the smaller one was easier to manage. After putting Derek's dressing gown on, we sat him in the chair and covered him over with a blanket, making sure the catheter bag was secure on his lap, and off we went with Gary pushing the chair.

When we arrived at the cafeteria, we found everything still closed. Gary looked out of the doors to see the sun was shining, so he suggested we take Derek for a walk to get some fresh air.

Outside there were several people standing around smoking, so Gary pushed the chair further along and just kept walking. On the right-hand side was the car park and the first thing Derek asked was, "Where is your car parked?"

I looked at Gary and shook my head. Gary realized what I meant and he quickly said, "Oh, we've come by the park and ride today, Dad, because there is a lot of traffic and the car park gets so full."

"That's a pity," Derek replied, "You could have taken me home."

Derek spoke about Gary taking him home several times during the walk. We could see Gary's car in the car park, but there were several others there, so Derek did not notice it, thank God.

A little further along on the left had been all brick weaved, with small areas of flower beds and wooden benches set around it. Some people were sitting enjoying the sunshine, but Gary kept walking. Because there were small, solid wheels on the chair, every time Derek spoke, his voice was all of a quiver and we started to laugh. As we turned the bend, we were then heading for the entrance to the hospital grounds and there was a keen wind blowing.

I pulled the blanket up closer around Derek's chest, and he said. "Are you pushing me home?"

The wind seemed so cool, I took off my jacket and put over Derek's' chest, making sure it covered him right up to his chin. The last thing I wanted was for him to catch a cold.

We knew where we were, as we had walked the same stretch of ground the night Derek had been admitted. It just seemed to go on and on. As Gary came to the edge of the pavement, it sloped down to make easy wheelchair access, and different coloured slabs had been used with little bumps on them. Every time Gary pushed the chair over these bumps, Derek kept saying, "Bloody hell!" The more we walked, the more we laughed.

We got to the end of the building and turned left making our way to the main entrance of the hospital, and I for one was pleased to get through the doors out of the cool wind.

We were all ready for a hot drink. The others sat down at a table while I went and fetched the hot drink. Derek was still making us all laugh about how rough his walk had been. We all chose something to eat and then pushed Derek back to the ward. After helping Derek back on the bed, we left so he could have his afternoon rest.

Gary and Anna were going to Ely to have a walk along the river, so I told them to leave because I had bought my reading book along and I would go and sit on one of the benches we had passed earlier that morning, until it was time to go back to see Derek. They said they did not like leaving me, but I insisted they should go as the time would go by quickly and I would be fine. As their car left the car park, Gary gave a quick pip and waved as they passed by.

Although I got my reading book from my bag I did not even bother to open it, as I enjoyed sitting watching the world go by.

I was miles away, thinking how much longer Derek would have to stay here, when a lady's voice asked me for the time and then asked if I minded her joining me on the bench. We sat and chatted about whom we had come to visit and where we both lived, and it was quite an enjoyable hour. The lady was alone, and I think she just wanted someone to talk to. We walked back through the corridor together and then went our separate ways.

Back on the ward, Derek was still lying on the bed and said he had had a sleep. I asked if he would like to go and sit in the garden, because Stuart and Caroline were bringing the children later this afternoon and we would all be able to sit together.

So, after the tea trolley came round and he had had his cup of tea, I once again got him ready for another walk but told him this one would be a lot smoother than the last time.

For a while, we sat on the chairs in the food-hall area, so that everyone had to walk by us to get to the wards. We would not miss Stuart, Caroline, and the children coming in. We sat for some time, when I decided I would go outside and ring Stuart to tell him we would be in the garden. Derek did not want to be left, so I pushed him outside and rang Stuart's mobile. Caroline answered and said they were about twenty minutes away. I told her to head for the garden when they got here.

It was lovely sitting on the bench in the garden. The sun was very warm, and the tall buildings surrounding the garden sheltered us from the chilly wind.

I asked Derek if he would like an ice cream, and he nodded and said, "I'll have a lolly." So I made sure he was OK, and then I headed back to the shop for the ice cream.

Because it was hot, the lolly melted rapidly. It ran down Derek's chin and onto the blanket. Once I had eaten mine, I helped Derek with his, just as all the family arrived. So, off I went back to the shop to get them all an ice cream, taking two grandchildren with me to help me carry them.

Once it started to turn chilly, Stuart and Caroline took Derek back to the ward while I stayed with the children.

Derek's two sisters, Heather and Shirley, brother Colin, and brother-in-law Chris arrived, and we let them sit with Derek for a while, as I had been at the hospital all day and Stuart and Caroline had been there a long while.

We sat in the cafeteria with the children until visitors' time was nearly over, and I popped back to the ward to say goodnight.

As I left Derek sitting in the chair, he once again asked if he could go with me. When I said it was not possible he said, "No, you don't want me home do you? Don't want to have to look after me do you?"

How do you explain to someone with a head injury the reason why he has got to stay in hospital? It really broke my heart to think he had this opinion of not being able to come home—blaming me!

The whole family had met in the cafeteria, and we sat and chatted. Colin paid for us all to have a hot drink for the adults and a cold drink for the children, and then we left since we were the only ones left sitting in there.

After I got home, I decided I would be up early in the morning and cook something to take to Derek and to see if the flask did keep the food hot.

I took some stewing steak from the freezer and put it in the fridge to thaw out overnight.

I was getting quite used to my daily routine now. I had to try and fit jobs in before and after my hospital visits, but if washing or ironing got behind I knew it would get done at some stage. Then, I was off to bed.

CHAPTER 28
Sunday, April 15

I was up at five thirty and the meat had thawed, so I cut it into very small pieces and cooked it in gravy with onions in the oven for two and half hours. While that was cooking, I prepared some potatoes, and then I peeled and cooked some apples and defrosted some blackberries I had picked from the hedgerow at the back of the house. I made some crumble mixture to put on the top of the fruit, so by nine thirty I had a steak pie made and baked. I cut a slice out and wrapped it in tin foil. The potatoes were boiled and mashed in the flask, with some peas and thick gravy. I made a custard and poured it over a portion of apple and blackberry crumble that was already in a plastic container and wrapped in tin foil. I packed it all in a shopping bag ready to take for Derek.

I was already and waiting for Sue to pick me up.

Derek was surprised when I told him what I had in the bag. We sat in the ward talking with him until Sue left, and then I produced a plate and spoon. As yet, Derek was not able to use a knife and fork, because with his swollen hand he was still unable to grip anything.

The potatoes, peas, and gravy were still hot from the flask, and when I unwrapped the pie, Derek's eyes lit up. I used the spoon to cut up the pie and passed Derek the spoon, He started to eat but was like a toddler trying to feed himself for the first time with gravy running down his chin and potatoes and peas falling on his lap. In the end, I had to tell him to steady up as his was hardly chewing his food before he shoved another very over-full spoonful in his mouth. I was scared he was going to choke.

After the main course, he started on the crumble and custard. The custard was running down his chin. His cheeks puffed out like a hamster, because he had shoved so much food in his mouth.

I had to stop his hand from pushing more food in his mouth and said, "Derek! What are you doing?"

He replied, "The doctor might come round and tell me I can go home."

I said, "Oh, Derek, the doctor will not be round today. It's Sunday and unless it's an emergency they don't do ward rounds."

He ate all the food I had taken in, so it was very satisfying to have gotten up early and to know for the first time Derek had enjoyed a meal.

I had taken some baby wipes and was able to clean him up; I was pleased the meal was over, because I thought he was going to choke.

Visiting time was over until two thirty, so I made my way to the cafeteria for a cup of tea and a muffin. I really did not fancy anything else and made my way outside to the benches I had sat on the day before, as the weather was dry but not as sunny or warm.

When I arrived back on the ward, Derek was holding his tummy. I asked if he was all right, and he said his tummy ached.

I said, "Let me take you to the toilet."

"No!" he replied, "I might miss the doctor."

I told him the doctor had gone, as I had met him then going out of the ward. I hadn't, but at least that kept Derek happy.

I finally managed to persuade him to go to the toilet, with me walking by his side. By the time we got to the loo, it was too late. After cleaning him up, I had to change his pyjama bottoms, but the nurse had once again put the tube to the catheter bag down the inside his pyjama leg, with the urine bag out of the bottom of his trousers. Because the bag was quite full, I had no idea how to get it through the leg of the pyjamas without unscrewing the tube from the bag and there was no way I was going to do that. I told Derek to keep still while I went to find a nurse.

A nurse was at the desk but was on the telephone, obviously waiting for someone to answer the other end. She asked how she could help, and after I explained, she said she would be there in a minute. So, back I went, and Derek was clinging onto the rails on each side of the toilet. So, while waiting for the nurse, I decided to flush the loo to alleviate the smell. All of a sudden, Derek gasped for breath and groaned and went death white.

"Oh, Derek, whatever is the matter?" I asked.

He whispered, "It's cold. It's cold."

I could not make out what was wrong until I glanced into the toilet and saw that the water had risen right to the top of the bowl and realized Derek had gotten a cold bidet. Well, at least his undercarriage had been washed. He didn't have the strength to pull himself off the toilet to get out of the way of the water.

When the nurse arrived and I explained what I had done, we both had a laugh, but Derek could not see the funny side of it. The nurse said that now Derek was able to walk to the toilet, they would be removing the catheter tomorrow.

After clean pyjama trousers and Derek feeling better, we headed back for the ward.

At the end of visiting time, I asked Derek if he would like me to bring in some more steak pie and potatoes for his lunch tomorrow.

His reply was, "Cor, yes please," so that was tomorrow's menu sorted.

I really cannot remember who came to visit that evening and obviously gave me a lift back.

Once home, I washed the dishes and flask, ready for tomorrow when I would refill them again.

I was amazed how tired I was every night now, either because I was more relaxed knowing Derek was gradually improving or because of how warm it was sitting in the hospital for so many hours.

CHAPTER 29
Monday, April 16

I was up early again this morning but that never, ever bothered me. I always got up the minute Derek left for work. I wanted to be ready for another long day ahead.

Once again I had cooked potatoes and mashed them until creamy, cooked some runner beans from the freezer, and heated another piece of steak pie, which I had only made on a small tea plate, just enough for three days unless Derek got fed up with it.

Stuart had gotten Derek a couple of pairs of jogging bottoms the day before, so I would take them and let Derek get dressed that day. It might make him feel a step closer to getting home.

Sylv came to pick me up, and away we went. En route I tried to explain to her, as we got closer to Cambridge, directions for her to take on her journey home—how many roundabouts, which ones to keep going straight over, and then once you go under a railway bridge at the next roundabout turn right. My sister gets lost wherever she goes.

When our Mum was in Addenbrookes, which I explained in the beginning of this book, Sylv drove her car there as we staggered our visits. If I took one sister during the afternoon, Sylv would take another sister at night or vice versa. I had explained to Sylv where to go, and when she left the hospital, she turned the wrong way and ended up in Newmarket.

So, she kept saying yes and would repeat after me where to go when she left the hospital after visiting Derek.

The catheter—at last—had been removed before we got there. I took Derek to the bathroom where I helped him to put some underpants and his jogging bottoms on and a clean top. He looked a different person: more human.

Once again, we took Derek to the cafeteria and had a cup of drink. We sat at the table saying to Derek what to say if the doctor came round and asked what day it was or what hospital he was in or what year it was. We kept testing him, and we made him keep repeating it, so hopefully he would get it right. But all he was really interested in was saying, "Take me home, get me out of here, sneak me out", so it would be very hard for me once I was on my own with him.

We walked back to the ward and gave him his dinner, which once again he enjoyed but would not eat the crumble as he said it would give him tummy ache. Once the bell sounded for the visitors to leave, I walked back to the car with Sylv and asked if she knew where to go. Very confidently she said, "Yes!"

Once she left the car park and was out of sight, I went back to the shop and bought some lunch and sat at a table to eat it. Then I got a cup of drink before I went back to the ward.

I had not been sitting down for long when the doctor and his students were doing their rounds. They walked to the bed next to Derek's, and all the while they were at this bed Derek kept saying, "Go on ask them if I can come home. Go on."

I said, "All right, Derek, wait until they come over here."

As soon as they approached the bed, I could see the anxiety on Derek's face, so before they had chance to say anything I asked if Derek could come home, because he was only sitting in the chair, which he could do just as well at home. Once again, the doctor shook his head. He looked at Derek and asked Derek what hospital he was in. Derek replied again, "Cambridge eye hospital."

The Three Birds

The doctor said he could be dangerous. He could climb out of a window, and I would not know. He could walk out the door onto the street and get lost, or he could hurt a family member. He then walked off with all his followers trailing behind.

A few minutes later, the doctor's PA came back and sat on the bed and was trying to convince both of us why Derek could not go home.

And then, she said to Derek, "Why are you squinting?"

He said, "So I can see you better."

"Oh, I'll make a note of it and get you an appointment with the eye specialist here.

She said, "You will be transferred to King's Lynn hospital where you will have rehabilitation before you can go home."

He looked so sad; he looked at me and said, "That's that then."

(To this day, he never did get an appointment for that eye clinic, but his sight got better after a time.)

Each day, I would sit and massage Derek's hand, as the fingers were still swollen and were all slightly bent.

The porter came to take him to the gym, where he did his usual exercises and the physio remarked on how Derek was now dressed and looking much better. I would have liked to walk him back to the ward on my own, but I could not remember the way back the physio had taken a few days earlier and there would be a lot of visitors and day patients walking the corridor during the day the way I would go, so I let the porter take him back.

Because Derek was now eating home-cooked food he did not want much from the food trolley when it came round. I would sometimes get him a pudding and custard or sometimes pop to the shop to buy him a rice pudding or jelly or even a packet of crisps, as long as he was now eating, because he had so much weight to put back on.

Gary and Anna came that night, so I once again disappeared to the cafeteria. There were different people to talk to and strike up new conversations. Although I spent every day sitting by Derek's bedside, conversation was limited at times. Yet, when I was away from him, sitting in the cafeteria or going for a wander round, I could not wait to get back to the ward to see him.

Whatever the outcome, I had been lucky, as I still had a husband.

On the way home, Gary and Anna thought Derek much more improved and not rambling on tonight, but because they said how he would not get into a conversation but kept crazing to get out of hospital. Gary was concerned how Derek would react when he realized he would have to stay at our local hospital and would not be coming home yet.

Now at the beginning of the day, I said how I explained to my sister, Sylv, how to get back home from Addenbrookes. Well, I will have to mention it now, but three and half years later when I was out with my three sisters having a meal, Sylv confessed at that point, that the day she left me at Addenbrookes she took the wrong turning and was heading for London. *Yes, London.* She had to stop at a garage and ask the way to Cambridge. The assistant explained, and she ended back at Cambridge and started off again. She left me at 1.00 p.m. and arrived home at nearly five o'clock. The journey from Addenbrookes to Sylva's home would normally take approximately sixty minutes, depending on the traffic, so where had she been for the other three hours? No one knows; not even Sylv.

CHAPTER 30
Tuesday, April 17

Today, I had taken him the last of the steak pie wrapped in tin foil and potatoes and butter beans in the flask and, as always, would get him a dessert from the hospital trolley, or if there was nothing he liked, I would go and get him something from the shop.

Stuart had come with me, and as usual we had taken Derek for a cup of tea in the cafeteria. We still pushed him in the wheelchair for now, as we did not want to exhaust him to soon. It was very busy, and there must have been lots of outpatient clinics. Once we had a drink, we pushed him to the garden, but it was chilly out there, so we decided to take him back to the ward as there was no way I was going to let him catch a cold after going through weeks trying to get him well.

Once we got back to the ward, I heard the food trolley arrive and went to get a plate from it and the man in charge of the food said, "What have you brought him in today, Mam?"

He laughed when I said it was the last of the steak pie. He said as long as he was eating and enjoying it. But still, Derek was trying to shove as much food in his mouth as he could. As soon as the spoon was empty, he put some more on it and then put it in his mouth before he had chewed the last lot.

Stuart had to say to him, "Steady up, Dad, or you will choke."

We talked about the grandchildren and what antics they were getting up to, but all Derek just kept saying was "Oh".

I asked if he could remember who I was talking about, and he shook his head from side to side. So, I sat and went through all their names and tried to describe them one by one, but I am sure he could not place any of them.

Stuart kept reminding him of the times they would all get Granddad on the floor and one by one jump on him and all end up in a big heap, and then one of them would ruffle his hair up and thought that was hilarious to see his hair all sticking up, but that still did not jog his memory

The sound of the bell rang along the corridor for the visitors to leave so the patients had their rest.

I told Derek I was going for something to eat and would be back very soon.

Stuart said his goodbyes as he would have to leave since he was on the afternoon shift and had to get back to get ready for work.

We walked back out to the car together, and Stuart left. I went back in and got some lunch. Time seem to drag when you sat on your own, but I did not mind. I sipped my cup of tea, but because I liked to drink it hot, once I had drank it I was ready to leave.

I cleared the table and put the rubbish in the bin and wandered slowly back round the shops and made my way back to the ward.

I never bothered to use the lift when I was on my own, only when I had Derek with me pushing him in the wheelchair. On reaching the outer doors of the ward, which were still locked, there were a couple of other visitors standing waiting for them to be opened. A conversation would always start up about something or another. When it was visitors' time once again, the lights along the dark corridor were switched on and you saw nurses preparing to do their duties once again. A nurse made her way to unlock the doors, and we would all troop through to see our relatives.

Once I sat down, I asked Derek if he would like to go to the garden, but he shook his head no and said he had to go to the gym, which I had completely forgotten about.

Every time I heard a wheelchair approaching I would say, "Here he comes to get you," but the porter would either go to another patient or pass the bay completely.

I sat asking Derek about the Elvis shows he had performed and the different charities we had raised money for and all the different jump suits he owned, and he looked at me and said, "I honestly don't know what you are talking about. I really can't remember them at all."

That really did scare me, as performing those shows always gave Derek an adrenalin boost.

The porter arrived to take Derek to the gym, and I walked at the side of them and made conversation, asking the porter how long he had been working at the hospital and how many people altogether worked at the hospital. I seem to remember him saying in all 6,000 members of staff. *Wow*, I was glad I didn't have to pay their wages.

It was a male physiotherapist that day because the young lady who had been helping Derek had moved to another department. He asked Derek to do the exercises he had been doing on previous days and concentrated more on his leg muscles to try and strengthen them. Derek looked so weak and thin, one could not help looking and try to imagine what was going through Derek's head. It was all very well, telling him about his previous life before the accident, but if he could not remember, it must be so confusing for him to try and understand everything we keep trying to explain to him.

Back on the ward, he said his legs ached after using them a lot in the gym. I suggested lying on the bed, but he said no.

I don't think the doctor did his rounds that day. All the days seem to be the same. I did make notes, but only really gentle reminders as to when Derek slept a lot, ate, etc.

A voice then spoke from behind me, and it was a couple of friends from the Elvis team came to see Derek. They sat with us for about an hour before they left.

It was soon time for that food trolley to reappear again with the patients' tea, and I could hear that familiar voice humming one of Elvis's songs. I knew it was the usual man on duty serving the food. I got some chips for Derek, as he had had a hot lunch and he was not very hungry, and some sponge pudding and custard. I helped him to eat the chips, as he kept saying he had had enough of them, but he enjoyed his sponge pudding and custard.

No matter what conversation I tried to have with Derek, the same thing kept being repeated, "When can I come home?" and I kept saying the same thing back to him, "When the doctor says you can."

The look on his face was either one of anger or despair, I'm not sure which.

Derek's mate, Mike, came to see him, and I was relieved that Derek could make a conversation with someone else. I knew in my heart of hearts he blamed me for not taking him home, but what else could I do?

I sat having some tea and began to wonder myself how long would Derek have to stay here. Every day we were told they had not heard of a bed at King's Lynn hospital, but I really was dreading it when they told Derek he would have to stay there for a while.

On my return to the ward he seemed to be having a right old chin wag and I sat letting the two mates talk away.

All too soon, it was time to leave as the dreaded bell had gone off, and I kissed Derek goodnight and told him I would be back in the morning.

He replied, "OK", and as I walked away he asked if I would take him with us. I was too choked to answer. I just shook my head, waved, and walked away with tears streaming down my face.

I would have loved nothing better than to be able to take him home with me; to look across the lounge and see him sitting there; sitting opposite him at the dinner table; or to hear him gently snoring lying next to me in bed. If only he knew.

CHAPTER 31
Wednesday, April 18

The girls took me again this morning. One of my sisters came to the ward, and once again we pushed Derek to the cafeteria and all sat round the table laughing and talking. Derek was very alert this morning and did not seem to be confused at all. Each of us in turn kept telling him the date, the hospital, and what accident he had had, just in case the doctors did their rounds later in the day. We kept asking him to repeat the answers to the questions, which to our amazement he did without thinking about it. So that in itself was a great improvement.

Around noon, I pushed him back to the ward so I could get him some food, which I had brought in with me, before the visitors' bell sounded. The trolley was already outside in the corridor and a different guy was serving the food today. He smiled and asked what could he get me. I smiled and said just a plate and some cutlery, as I had already bought some food from home. He told me to help myself. I said I would come back to get Derek some pudding, once I had gotten him eating his main course.

This morning, I had been up early and made a sausage pie. I made the pastry and then stripped the sausage meat from the skins and rolled the meat flat to fit onto the pastry at the bottom of the plate and then covered it with pastry over the top and baked it.

In the good, old, trusty flask I had potatoes cooked earlier, along with some runner beans from the freezer, and had made the gravy. His face lit up when I opened the tin foil and laid a large helping of the tart on the plate and then the vegetables and gravy.

He ate it as though he had not seen food for days, while I went back to the trolley to get a dessert for him. When I arrived back at the bedside, all the tart was gone, and he was finishing the vegetables. Once again, I had to stress if he carried on like that he would choke, but he said again the doctor might come round and say he can go home with me.

Once he had finished his food, I cleaned up his face and hands with some baby wipes, and he needed a clean top because he had spilt some of the food down it.

The tea lady arrived, and Derek had asked for a cup of tea just as the bell sounded for the visitors to leave. So making sure he could reach his drink all right, I left to go and sit and have my lunch as usual.

As I arrived back to the ward, the porter came to take Derek to the gym for his usual exercises, and once again I walked with them. There seemed to be several patients in the gym today. The young man came and walked Derek to a bed and did several leg-muscle exercises with him and also gave him a small ball to squeeze in his right hand. His fingers were still like fat sausages, but the cut had healed up smashing.

I asked the physio at the end of the session if I could walk Derek back to the ward myself on foot and not in the wheelchair, and he said if I was sure I could manage him on my own it would do him good, so off we went.

We walked slowly and kept to one side of the corridor so we were not in any one's way. I pressed for the lift to take us to the ward instead of taking the stairs. As we walked through the doors into the ward, there were shouts of encouragement coming from the nurses, and Derek's face lit up to think he had actually walked from the gym to the ward, although he was eager to sit down once back by his bed.

He said it had made his legs ache and he had missed his afternoon drink, but I could hear the trolley further along the ward, so I went to get him a cup of tea.

I said now we knew he was feeling stronger and more confident on his legs, we could perhaps walk to the garden tomorrow without the wheelchair.

Soon after we arrived back on the ward the doctor came into the room and came straight to where we were sitting. He asked Derek what the date was, did he know what hospital he was at, and lastly what his date of birth was. At last, Derek gave all the correct answers. The doctors were pleased with him, and said they still had not heard when they would be transferring him to King's Lynn.

Derek then asked, "Can I go home doctor?"

The doctor's replied, "You have improved from the last time I saw you, but we cannot let you home as yet. You will have to wait until a bed becomes available at King's Lynn hospital."

The doctor then walked to the patient in the bed opposite.

I could see the disappointment on Derek's face but cheered him up by saying at least they could see how much better he could walk, and as each day passed, he would get stronger and soon be home.

A couple of friends walked in at that moment and were able to chat about different topics, so that seem to put him in a good mood, and he never mentioned about going home for the rest of their visit.

I really cannot remember who came to pick me up that night, as in my diary I had just roughly written daily events down that concerned Derek as a patient, so please forgive me if you were the one who came to visit Derek that night and give me a lift home.

CHAPTER 32

Thursday, April 19

A friend, Shirley, also member of the Elvis team, offered to take me to the hospital today, and of course she wanted to visit Derek, so off we went. Traffic was not too heavy that morning, and we soon arrived at the hospital and parked.

I was a little taken aback when I walked into the bay this morning. Derek was still in bed, and he had not had a shave and basically looked a mess.

After we both greeted him, I asked him if he had had a shower, and he said no. As we sat talking to him, a young nurse came into the room, and I asked her why hadn't Derek had a shower, and she replied that he had earlier that morning and she left.

I looked back at him, and he said. "I haven't had a shower today."

I knew he still had his pyjamas on from yesterday and not had a shave.

So, Derek remained in bed all the time of the morning visit. After Shirley had left at lunch time, I made Derek sit on the edge of the bed and pushed his table up close to him, and I gave him his lunch of sausage tart, mashed potato, and baked beans, which he really enjoyed. I had also taken a tub of rice pudding that I had gotten from the shop the night before. He enjoyed his lunch and was not half as messy as other days.

After the bell sounded, I made my way to the cafeteria. After I had purchased a salad from the shop, it was very busy in there, so I got a cup of tea and made my way outside to sit on a garden seat in the paved area opposite the car park where previous days I had gone. Very few people ventured that far to have their cigarettes so there was always a seat available. Although the sun was shining there was a cool breeze, but by finding the right spot in the garden, you were sheltered. A young mother sat feeding her baby with a bottle of milk on one seat. On another sat a middle-aged man reading a book and a couple of elderly people sat at the far end, I decided to go and join them because it was the most sheltered spot, but as I sat down they got up. The lady remarked that they were not being rude by leaving just as I got there, but that she had an outpatient appointment and was unable to walk very quickly, so they wanted to make sure they were not late for it.

After I had eaten and drunk my tea, I sat and watched the world go by until it was time to go back to the ward.

I had just got back to the bedside, when another young nurse came into the room, and I asked if I could give Derek a shower as he had not had one. On producing a piece of paper from her pocket, she remarked she had only just come on duty and was aware that all the patients had had a shower earlier that morning.

I said, "Well, this one hasn't."

She said she would go and ask. Minutes later, a sister appeared by the bed and apologized. Derek had not had a shower as they were short staffed on the morning shift. I asked if I could give him a shower, and the sister said if I could manage it would be a great help to them. At that moment, the porter came to take Derek to the gym, but he said to carry on what I was doing and to get my husband showered. He had another patient to collect and would come back for Derek in an hour.

Firstly, I got Derek's electric razor and gave him a shave while he was sitting on the bed. I then collected Derek's wash bag and towel, along with his clothes, and he climbed from the bed and off we went to the shower room.

It was a large, tiled room with a shower in the corner, with a white plastic seat for the patient to sit on and a plastic curtain to pull across once in the shower. Two more chairs stood against the wall on the opposite side, where you could put your clothes to keep them dry, and there were two wash basins on the same wall. I locked the door, then undressed Derek and sat him on the seat. I turned the shower head away from him while I turned the shower on and made sure the water was the correct temperature. I wetted him up, washed his hair, and then washed him down from head to foot. He was very unsteady standing on his own, but he held on to me while I washed the lower regions and the backs of his legs. Once I had dried his top half and put a tee shirt on him, I then walked him over to the dry area in the room and sat him on a chair, which I had already draped a towel over, and dried his lower half. Once he was dressed, I cleaned his teeth and combed his hair.

As we emerged from behind locked doors, with Derek holding on to my right arm for support, I suddenly felt wet and looking down saw the front of my trousers and top were soaked, as were my sandals.

A nurse walked by, smiled, and said, "Which one of you had the shower, then?" causing us all to laugh.

Once we got back to his bedside, Derek sat in his chair, and I went and found another one to sit on. Minutes later, one of the research team walked into the room and came over to Derek to ask if he would mind having another MRI scan the next morning. They always had to ask the patient, just in case the patient wanted to opt out anytime from helping the research team. Derek said it would be no problem. She stayed talking for about twenty minutes and then left when the porter returned to take Derek to the gym.

When we got back to the bedside, Derek said he had a slight headache so I made him lay on top the bed, and in no time at all he was asleep.

I sat looking at a book when the occupational therapist arrived and stood talking.

She said, "You know, Mrs Russell, he has done remarkably well, but you must realize he will be at the rehabilitation centre at King's Lynn for many weeks to come."

I asked if I could take him there on a daily basis, and she shook her head and said, "I'm afraid not."

She said she would come back a little later when Derek was awake.

Who would think it could turn out such a busy day? Soon after, Derek woke and said his headache had gone and he felt fine. He then sat in the chair and had a cup of tea (amazing he still asked for tea and not his favourite cup of coffee). I walked him to the toilet, and when we got back the occupational therapist came back and sat on the bed and did various tests with Derek asking him questions. Afterwards, she said he had scored nine out of ten, which was very good. Before she left, she said if he was not transferred, she would most likely come and see him again.

A patient was then being pushed by in his bed to another bay, and a voice called out, "Are you all right, Elvis?"

It was the male nurse, Nick, who had asked me to help him wash Derek's hair on the critical-care ward. On his way back through the corridor, he popped his head in and told Derek he was looking good. Nick asked how I was feeling and said he could not stop as they were very busy, and he was gone.

I did not realize the time had flown by. The evening meal was being served in the next bay. You got to know the rattling sound of the trolley. Once again, I related to Derek what was on the menu, but all he wanted was the treacle pudding and custard. No sooner had he eaten that when Gary walked in. After a few minutes it was my cue to leave for something to eat, and it did Derek good to have a break from me.

On the way home, Gary thought his dad looked much better and I relayed all the days' events to him, but I can tell you I felt shattered tonight and could not wait to get to bed. I think I was more relieved that I knew I could cope with Derek if he was to come home. When he first starting walking, and I could see how he was very unsteady on his feet and leaning to one side. The memory loss about the family worried me, but in time that might come back.

CHAPTER 33

Friday, April 20

My sister, June, and her husband, John, came to collect me today, and I gave them an update. There seemed to be a lot of traffic today, perhaps because it was Friday. We kept getting stuck behind tractors on the road moving from one field to another or a heavy-goods vehicle we were unable to overtake because of the bends in the road, but as long as we got to the hospital what did it matter? Better to be late than not at all.

We walked into the room, and Derek's first words were, "I'm being moved to Lynn."

"Oh," I replied, "are you? When?"

"In a minute I think," he said, "They've been in here to tell me."

I said, "At least it's a step closer to getting home."

A lady walked over and said, "Mrs Russell, Derek will be transferred to the Queen Elizabeth hospital today. I am just trying to locate someone who can tell me roughly what time the ambulance will be here. As soon as I know I will come and tell you."

Then, the dreaded words came from Derek, "Once I get to Lynn hospital, then I can come home, can't I?"

With that, I had to think quick and told him that he would perhaps have a few days there for them to assess you.

The lady returned with a folder in her hand and said that the ambulance would collect Derek at 1.00 p.m. I thanked her as she walked from the room.

"Oh, what about your MRI scan you are supposed to have today?" I asked.

Derek replied he had already had it early this morning, so that was out of the way.

With the lunch trolley approaching I went and got a plate and cutlery and once again emptied the contents of the flask onto the plate: mashed potato, vegetables and gravy, and sausage tart. He only picked at the food on the plate, and I knew he was getting worried about the ambulance men coming to collect him while he was still eating. He did not want any pudding, but he did drink a cup of tea.

Once the food was disposed of, I packed Derek's belonging in a bag so he was ready for the off. I said that I would take home the books I had taken for him to look at and sort out some different ones to take to the hospital later, but he was constantly staring at the door waiting to be collected.

When the bell went for the visitors, I told Derek I would go back home with June and John and then make my way to King's Lynn hospital by 3.00 p.m.

We made our way home, and I was dropped off at the door. I let the two boys and other family members know what was happening and Keith, so he would not have to come round to feed the dogs as visiting times would be completely different to Addenbrookes. I knew I would be at home more. I made myself a cup of tea. I had already eaten, as my sister had taken some of my favourite egg sandwiches and we had eaten them before we left the car park at Cambridge.

It felt so strange sitting behind the wheel of the car once again as it had been five weeks that I had been chauffeured around. I made sure I had plenty of change for the car park, and off I set. As I drove past the bungalow where June and John lived, I gave them a blast on the horn to let them know I was on my way.

Once I arrived at the car park and found a space, I thought the best place to ask where Derek would have been admitted to was, perhaps, the physiotherapy reception area.

I stood for a few minutes as the receptionist was making an appointment for the man in front of me, and then, I was about to speak, the telephone rang. Feeling eager to find where Derek was, I must have sighed louder than I should have done.

The young lady looked up and whispered, "Sorry to keep you waiting."

Once off the phone, she gave me her full attention as I explained the events of the previous hours. She asked a colleague sitting at a desk behind her where I would most likely find my husband.

Then, she picked up the telephone and said, "I'll see if I can find him for you."

"No luck there," she said. "I'll try another ward."

"No, he's not there. What ward did you say he was in at Addenbrookes? I'll ring them to find out who contacted them regarding a bed."

She put the phone down and then scrolled through a sheet of paper and then rang another number.

After five different phone calls, she smiled and put the receiver down and said, "Your husband is in Terrington ward."

I exclaimed, "Terrington ward! But that's the old people's ward. My mum was in there."

She then directed me to a shortcut through the corridors from the physiotherapy area, and I made my way to the ward.

On arrival there, I asked the nurse at the desk where I would likely to find Derek. She looked at some notes and said he had not arrived yet.

I said, "Perhaps that explains why no one could find out for me which ward he was in."

She pointed to a chair and said that I could wait until he arrived, so I sat and wondered how long I would have to wait.

I glanced in the bay that I was sitting outside, and one man just inside was lying on the bed talking to the man in the bed opposite. The curtains were pulled round the next bed. Near the window on the opposite side was an elderly man who looked very poorly, and in the centre bed, sitting beside it, was a very large man in shorts with very swollen red legs, but he seemed very chirpy.

A nurse appeared through the curtains that were round the centre bed, and she quickly pulled them back to reveal my very distraught husband. Derek had been there all the time!

As I approached the bed, he looked at me and said, "Where ever have you been? I've sat here ages."

I then repeated to him the afternoon's events and that no one could find which ward he was in.

By this time visiting was over, so I left with a heavy heart as Derek said, "Can I come with you now?"

I said I would be back later after I had fed the dogs. The look on his face said it all.

On my way home, I stopped at an electrical store and got Derek a DVD player with a screen so that he could watch a film on it, although, as in Addenbrookes, there was a TV and telephone above the bed. The man in the next bed was watching his TV, but there was no way I could get a prepaid card for the TV above Derek's bed because that would also give him access to the telephone and he could start ringing all sorts of people up and causing problems.

As soon as I got home, I read the instructions as how to charge the battery up on the DVD player and plugged it in to charge. At least I had managed to get that right. I fed the dogs and got myself some food, and it was off back to the hospital armed with a couple of DVD's and the charged player.

I walked into the bay, and Derek was chatting with the man in the next bed, so at least that was a good sign.

I produced the DVD player and gave him instructions on how to load it and what buttons to press. It started to play one of the latest Elvis shows. Once I had shown him a couple of times how to switch it on and off, I said he could watch it after I had gone home.

The man in the next bed had a lady visitor, and we kept joining in each other's conversation. Later, he introduced the visitor as his wife. I felt more at ease. At least Derek had someone to talk to after visiting was over. Derek kept expressing what an awful journey it was from Addenbrookes to King's Lynn. The ambulance was the roughest ride he had ever had and the longest it seemed.

He said the man opposite kept talking about sport all the time, especially football, which Derek cannot stand; he only really enjoys Formula 1.

With visiting only from 6.45 p.m. until 8.00 p.m. on this ward in the evening, it was time to leave. I left some money with Derek in case he wanted to buy something from the trolley when it came round the next morning. There always used to be a voluntary worker came round the ward every morning pushing a trolley containing newspapers, confectionary, and toiletries.

Derek insisted that I should take the DVD player home with me. I tried to persuade him he could watch it to make the night go quicker, but he was having none of it, getting annoyed with me and saying, "Take it!"

So, to keep the peace, I took it home with me.

I just hoped he'd be more settled tomorrow as we didn't know how long he would be there for.

I would feel lost tomorrow as I would be at home longer than usual because visiting times were much shorter at this hospital.

CHAPTER 34
Saturday, April 21

I woke up and suddenly remembered I didn't have to make that journey to Cambridge that morning.

It seemed such a long time since I had time to spend at home, I just wandered about. I made a cup of tea and sat looking out of the window. I kept thinking about all that had happened over the last five weeks. It was like being trapped in a dream and, no matter which way you went, you just could not get out of it. My thoughts were then interrupted when a voice called out. It was Sylv, who came round once more. I made her a drink, and then Keith appeared to take the dogs for a walk.

I asked if he was sure about taking the dogs now that I was at home more, and he said he was getting some good exercise by walking, otherwise he never walked anywhere, so off he went. Sylv left soon afterwards to go home for her breakfast of porridge.

Later on that morning, I remembered I had a letter to post, so I backed the car out of the garage and went to post it. On my return, I unlocked the door, and as I stepped inside the kitchen, I heard the floor boards creaking above. I suddenly froze. I thought someone was moving about upstairs. I stood and listened as the creaking went on and on. What should I do—phone someone or go upstairs? It went all quiet for a moment, and it started up again. Keith was still out with the dog, my bodyguard, so I had not got her in the house or come to that no burglar would have dared face her, as she was a large dog.

Had I forgotten to lock the back door before I went to post my letter? No, of course not, because I remembered unlocking it when I came home. Then, the noise started up again. This time, I felt more confident. I went back to the back door and turned the key and hid it behind a plant on the window sill. If anyone was in the house, they weren't going to get out through the door.

Slowly and silently I went up the stairs, my heart thumping like mad and my mouth dry. I stood on the landing. There was silence once again, save for the thudding in my chest.

I quietly opened the first door I came to, which was the front bedroom. Nothing unusual in there, so I closed the door. Then, I slowly pressed the door handle on the back bedroom door and opened it. All was quiet in there. I walked by the bathroom door and looked into our bedroom as the door was half way open—nothing in there. I opened the other back bedroom door and nothing in there.

Just as I turned round, the noise started again. I was trying hard to swallow, but my mouth was so dry. I thought my heart was going to jump out of my chest, but the bathroom being the only room I hadn't looked in.

I gently pressed the handle down and slowly opened the door. It would only open about six inches and then stopped. As I looked down I could see small pieces of glass under the door. I pushed a little harder, and the door opened a bit further. That was enough for me to get my head through the door, and I saw glass smashed in a large area of the floor.

Oh god, I thought, *someone's broken in through the window.*

Then, the noise started up again. As I made my way round the door, first I looked straight toward the window, but all panes of glass were intact. Then, as I slowly turned my head round behind the door, I could see what had happened: the shower door had completely shattered, just like a car wind screen goes

The Three Birds

when a stone hits it with force. Some of the toughened glass was falling in the shower tray and some falling outwards. Very tiny particles were breaking off from larger pieces. I could not believe what had happened.

Keith rang the doorbell as he wanted to let the dog in. I ran down stairs to unlock the door and tell him the story.

The telephone rang. It was Gary to ask what time would I be going to the hospital as he had the boys this weekend and he thought he would take them to see Granddad and cheer him up, so we arranged I would go to Gary's and leave the car there, and we could walk through the estate to the hospital, only five minutes away.

I had the task of clearing up the mess and it took some time, I can tell you. I could not believe how the time was passing so quickly. I made a sandwich and a cup of tea. I swept some glass up but looking at the clock I would have to finish it when I came back. Now I couldn't have a shower; I would have to have a bath.

I had just stepped out of the bath when the telephone rang again, so I went across the landing to the bedside table to answer it.

What a shock I got when I heard Derek's voice. He said, "Where are you? I've been waiting for you to come for ages."

I explained that visiting time was different to Cambridge and that I was then getting ready to come to see him.

He replied, "Well, hurry up 'cause I've got an escape plan. I'm getting out of here."

I began to panic, and I said, "Just sit on your bed, and soon as I put the phone down I'll leave and be with you right away."

A little, timid voice the other end, said, "OK, but hurry."

I dressed as quickly as I could and made straight for Gary's. I explained about the shower door and the call from his dad. We made the boys put their shoes on, and we set off.

Gary stayed with the boys in the restaurant area while I went to find Derek. There he sat in his bedside chair with his bag packed, ready on the bed. The nurse called me over and said that one of the other nurses had found him walking along the corridor with his bag and bought him back to the ward.

He looked a complete mess, very unusual for Derek. His face was all stubble, which he always hated, and his hair was a mess. The man in the next bed said he never got undressed last night, but just lay on the bed fully clothed. The nurses had tried to persuade him to get undressed, but he wouldn't have any of it. He was obviously going to try and escape in the night.

I could not imagine where he would have ended up if that nurse had not seen him.

All he kept saying was "Get me out of here. I'm not staying here. They are not carrying me out in a box."

He repeated that over and over again until I was near to tears. I told him I would go and get Gary. Once back in the sitting area, I explained to Gary what Derek was like and ask if he could go and calm him down. So, we all walked back into the ward, but Derek would not listen to us at all. He just kept repeating himself over and over. The more Gary tried to explain he could not just walk out of the hospital, the more determined he was to go.

We must have been there half an hour with him, then I had a thought. I went over to the nurse and asked if I could take Derek home for a couple of hours. She said she would have to go and ask the doctor, so off she went to find out.

Derek would not even speak to the boys. He just ranted and raved all the time. The nurse returned with a smile and said Derek could go but would have to be back on the ward by 6.00 p.m. I promised he would be, but I said that with little confidence. Once I got him out of the hospital would I get him back?

Back at the bed, I told him he could come home for a while but would have to come back later. He said, "OK."

Gary and the boys went back to their home, and Gary would drive our car round the front of the hospital to pick us up. We slowly walked to the main doors and waited for Gary to arrive. Derek sat in the front, and I climbed in the back with the two boys.

I was surprised at the conversation that struck up in the front of the car between Gary and his dad. Derek now seemed much calmer and turned round to talk to the boys in the back of the car.

We arrived home to find Stuart's car there, and he walked outside and a smile spread across his face when he saw his Dad.

Derek's first words were, "Thank god I've got out of there."

I quickly replied, "But you have got to go back, remember?"

Once inside the house, I opened the French doors. Because the garden was very secluded, it was warm and sunny out there. Derek walked through the open door straight into the garden. His dog was barking and whining, so I let him off his chain and he ran straight toward Derek and jumped up. Derek was fussing him, and it was very emotional to see.

I went into the kitchen to make a cup of tea; while the kettle was boiling I took my rocking chair out for Derek to sit on as I could see he was still very weak. He had walked from the ward to the front doors of the hospital.

First day back from the hospital

The boys went and had a look at the exploded shower door and said it was no problem to order another door, and Gary said he would ring round and get some prices on Monday morning for me.

I think I can remember making a cup tea for everyone, and then Gary said he would go back home and let Dad have a rest, then come back later to take him back to the hospital. Stuart said he would leave as well and gave Gary and the boys a lift back home so I would have the car to drive Derek back to the hospital.

I asked Derek if he would like a bath, and he replied, "Oh, yes please."

Once the bath was ready, I walked behind him up the stairs. I had already put a chair in the bathroom for him to sit on, and then I had to undress him and help him into the bath. He sat there like a small child while I bathed him and washed his hair. I helped him out of the bath and sat him on a chair to dry him, as he had very little strength.

Once downstairs, I dried his hair and then he lay down on the settee and went fast asleep. I crept around so as not to wake him, but the time seem to be flying by.

I thought what could I make for his tea that he would enjoy. I knew he loved homemade oven chips and a fried egg. Just as it was nearly ready, I went and gently nudged him to wake up. At first he wasn't sure where he was. Then he realized he was at home. Rather than set the table in the dining room, I had turned the oblong coffee table round so that I could sit in the armchair opposite Derek. We had always disliked sitting having our meals this way, but this was an exception.

Derek then said, "I'm sorry I went to sleep, but all I could hear were the birds singing in the garden and the ticking of an old-fashioned clock on the wall and I must have just drifted off."

He looked at the plate of egg and chips and said, "I don't feel hungry. I'm sorry, but I can't eat it."

"No problem," I told him, "I'll get you a cup of tea in a minute."

Out of the corner of my eye I saw him pick up the fork and stab it in a chip and eat it, then another and another, until he had eaten nearly everything, including the egg.

"That was lovely," he said.

I cleared the plates away without making any remarks and made a hot drink.

I dreaded the next speech I was about to make. It was nearly half past five, so I said, "Derek, I'll have to get you back to the hospital soon."

I was amazed when he said, "OK," and he went back with no problem at all.

Once he was sitting back in his chair in the hospital, the food trolley arrived, and it was obvious Derek did not want anything to eat. I said I would go and ask the nurse if you could come home again tomorrow, so he could have Sunday lunch with me. Again, she said she would go and ask the doctor on duty. Visiting time had nearly finished, when she came over and said I could collect Derek at 11.00 a.m. and get him back to the hospital by 3.00 p.m., so that cheered Derek up.

Derek asked me to leave him some more money as he had used nearly all the change I had left him to use the pay phone when he had telephoned me earlier.

Just as I was about to leave, I produced the DVD player with one of his concert recordings, and this time he said he would watch it.

I drove home feeling good, as I never expected in a million years that Derek would go back to the hospital like he did.

Once home drinking a cup of tea I thought I had nothing in the house to cook for Sunday lunch so I put my thinking cap on and thought I would leave earlier in the morning to go to the hospital but would go to a butchers to get some steak with some vegetables from the green grocers all under the same roof and then go to the hospital to collect Derek.

CHAPTER 35

Sunday, April 22

After going to the farm shop along the road for the meat and vegetables, I made my way to the hospital; I didn't want to be late, whatever happened.

When I arrived, he was already for me. Again, he had slept in his clothes, so after getting his clean jogging bottoms from his cupboard and his razor, etc., we made our way home. It wasn't so warm, so he would be unable to sit outside, but would be happy just sitting looking out of the window.

Although Derek seemed to be walking better, he was still very weak and everything was an effort for him. He sat in an armchair by the French doors watching the different birds on the feeder until I had cooked lunch. We sat at the dining table and both enjoyed our meal. This was the first time in over five weeks we had actually sat at the table and eaten a meal together. I made him a hot drink and told him to go and sit back in the other room while I cleared the dishes away.

When I waked back into the lounge, there was Derek lying down on the settee fast asleep. His mug of tea stood on the floor untouched. I crept upstairs and got a blanket to cover him up and just let him sleep.

I sat trying to read a book I had started way before Derek had his accident; everything seemed so quiet apart from the ticking of the clock on the wall.

As time seemed to be flying by, I had to wake Derek to tell him it would soon be time to go back to the hospital. He kept apologizing for falling asleep, but that did not bother me. At least he was getting his rest in, as he said he had another terrible night's sleep. After he had a cup of tea, I told him that before I took him back to the hospital we were going to get him cleaned up.

We went through the same process as the day before: bath, hair wash, and shave, and then all clean clothes on, and once again he looked very presentable. We headed back for the hospital.

I drove round the car park and parked. As we walked through the next row of cars, I recognized a blue MG classic car and thought that it belonged to a couple of friends who always supported our charity concerts and who had been in contact about the progress of Derek since the accident.

We had almost approached the double doors of the ward, when low and behold the couple sat on the seat waiting for our return. They had arrived to see Derek, and when the nurse explained where Derek was and what time he was expected to return they decided to wait and see him. We sat chatting for a while, and I suddenly realized I had not let the nurse on duty know Derek was back. I left Derek talking while I saw the nurse and told her Derek was sitting talking to some friends just outside the ward doors, she said that was fine.

It was long after visiting time was over that the friends left. Because we sat outside the doors to the ward I guess it did not matter. I then walked back with Derek to the ward; I said I would have to leave and come back later, which I did.

I had only been back in the ward a few minutes when more friends turned up to see Derek, and he seemed to be chatting to them as though he was enjoying his stay there. What would he be like when I left him? But again he accepted he would have to stay and seemed fine about it.

It was such a relief that I could walk away and go home without Derek making a fuss as I had expected him to.

What another great result today. It seemed to have settled Derek by being allowed to come home for those short visits, but how long would it be before he started to complain and make a fuss about coming home again?

CHAPTER 36

Monday, April 23

My first thoughts when waking up were that I wondered what sort of night's sleep Derek had had, as he slept soundly on the settee yesterday afternoon.

I busied myself about the house in the morning, and I took several telephone calls from family and friends enquiring after Derek. After I ate some lunch, I decided I would go and have a bath and then get ready for the hospital visit.

It was almost time to leave, so I grabbed the car keys and was just about to lock the door when I heard the telephone ring.

After I had said, "Hello," that familiar voice the other end said, "Hello, it's only me."

It was Derek.

I said, "Oh, I was just about to the lock the door and make my way to see you."

His reply was, "I think I can come home."

I said, "No, I don't think so."

He said, "Yes, I'm sure I can. The physiotherapist came round, and I had to walk up and down the ward. Then he said 'Would you like to go home?'"

"Well, Derek, I am just about to leave, so I will sort it out when I get there, OK?"

He replied, "OK."

What sort of visit was I in for today? I had not got the support of either son to call upon as they were both at work

Derek seemed in a good mood, but he was constantly watching for a member of the medical team to come over and tell him he could go home. He explained again how the physio had made him walk up and down and was really pleased with him.

By the time visiting was over, we had not seen anyone with any authority to ask. The nurse at the desk was constantly answering the telephone and organizing other members of staff. Finally, I did get to ask her, but she knew nothing about it. I told Derek that when I came back later I would ask to speak to someone then, he looked disappointed and said, "OK."

I did not really know what to make of the situation. If Derek was excited over nothing, it did not bear to think about. But we would have to deal with it later.

Back home after feeding the dogs, I made myself a meal and ate it. It must have been just after five o'clock when the telephone rang and a lady's voice asked to speak to Mrs Russell.

I said, "Speaking."

She said, "This is Doctor—[I cannot remember her name]. How would you like your husband to come home?"

"Why, of course. Yes," I said.

She then went on to ask several questions: was there anyone else living in the home apart from us two? would I be able to cope with him on my own? how would I get him home, etc.? With all questions answered, she then said that she was going to have a meeting with other doctors to decide as to whether they would allow Mr Russell home and she would ring me back. I told her that I planned to leave for the hospital around six o'clock, so if she rang and the answer phone cut in I would be making my way to the hospital. Would she come to the ward to speak to me? She assured me it would not be a problem. I put the phone down and just could not believe they were considering letting Derek home after being told he would be in rehabilitation for several weeks to come.

The Three Birds

I could not concentrate on anything, waiting for that phone to ring with an answer. Time was ticking by, and I would soon have to leave, as it usually took me twenty-five to thirty minutes to get to the hospital, depending on the traffic. I only had to get behind a large agricultural vehicle on our narrow country roads, and I could be stuck behind it until I got to King's Lynn.

The phone rang, and it was the lady doctor.

"We have decided that your husband can come home," she said, "Will you be able to take him home tonight?"

I thanked her very much and, putting down the receiver, I just stood amazed. Then I thought, *He's been in hospital five weeks. I'm going to get him out of there.*

I rang Gary and Stuart with the news because I did not want them to turn up at visiting time if we had already left.

I arrived on the ward and said, "You're coming home."

"See, I told you I could," was Derek's reply.

After clearing out his locker and packing everything in his bag, we were ready for the off, but the nurse said we had to wait for the doctor to give us Derek's discharge paper and a letter for our GP. Derek was not on any medication, so we did not have to wait for that.

We must have sat there half an hour when a doctor walked up to the nurses' desk and passed her an A4 sheet of paper and an envelope and left.

Then, the nurse called to me, "I've got them."

Derek said his goodbyes to the other patients. We both walked over to the desk where the nurse gave us the papers needed, and we were away.

It was a long walk down the corridors to the main entrance. I asked Derek if he wanted to sit down a minute.

He said, "No fear. I'm not going to sit down until I get in that car, in case they change their mind."

As we neared the entrance I told him to sit on a chair just inside the doors while I went to get the car, but he would not leave my side.

I think he was frightened that if I left him alone, I would not come back for him, so we slowly walked to the car. As luck should have it, I had parked in the first row right near the foot path.

As I drove home, he kept saying, "Thank god I'm out of there. I was determined they weren't going to carry me out of that hospital in a box, like they did all those others."

I asked what he meant, and he said the nurse would walk round and pull the curtains but he had a gap in his curtain and could see a trolley being pushed out of the ward with a corpse on it.

He said, "It happened five times since I have been in that ward, and it's not going to happen to me."

Did it really happen or was it just his imagination?

I said, "Never mind, you're going home."

He replied, "I'm not going back there, either."

(On reading the obituaries in the local paper over the next couple of weeks I discovered he was right)

Once home and he was settled in the armchair, I began to ring family members and friends to let them know that Derek was home at last.

I could see Derek was tired, so with all good intentions, off we went to bed. We both usually read for a little while, but once his head hit the pillow, he was asleep, so lights out. But I could not seem to drop off. It was like listening for a baby to wake. He began to toss and turn several times. I asked if he was all right.

He said, "I just can't get comfortable."

This went on another half an hour or so. I then suggested that we go back downstairs for a while, so dressing gowns on and back down stairs. I made a cup of tea and then suggested he try and go to sleep on the three-seater settee and I would lie on the two-seater settee. I went upstairs and came back down with pillows and blankets to make a bed up for Derek. My feet hung over the arm of the settee and felt most uncomfortable, but I did not care. I could hear Derek tossing and turning and now and again we would have a conversation and then lay quiet. One would think the other was asleep, but neither of us was. Perhaps we had a few cat naps but not sound sleep.

CHAPTER 37

Tuesday, April 24

I heard Derek yawn, and I whispered to him in case he was still a sleep, but he answered me, so I got up and made us both a drink. It was only five o'clock; it had been a long night

I put the bed clothes back up stairs. After I helped Derek to bathe himself, and then had some breakfast I told him to go and sit in the other room while I did a few jobs around the house, which he did. After a while, I went to check to see if Derek wanted a drink, but he was lying down on the settee fast asleep. So I pulled the door to and made myself a drink and sat down in the rocking chair in the dining room, as I did not want to disturb him.

Around mid-morning the telephone rang, and when I answered it a male voice said, "Hello, is that Mrs Russell?"

I replied, "Yes,"

"Oh, this is the occupational therapist from the Queen Elizabeth hospital. I was just calling to see how Derek is this morning."

I said that he was on the settee fast asleep. He said that's the best thing for him. He then went on to say that he thought he would progress quicker and better in his own surroundings than in hospital, as he seemed to be getting frustrated. He had passed all of Derek's details onto the neurological department and someone will contact me to make an appointment to call and see Derek. If there were any problems, I should give him a call. I thanked him for his help.

Derek then called out, "Who was that?"

I explained the conversation I had just had, when the doorbell rang, and it was my cousin calling to see Derek. After an half an hour, the doorbell went again, and some friends from the Elvis team came in. I made them all a cup of tea, and around mid-day they all left.

I escorted Derek to the toilet every time he needed to go. He was not strong enough as yet to stand to clean himself up, so without any fuss from either of us, I would do it for him. If he just wanted to relieve himself, he would have to sit down on the toilet to do it. He just hadn't got the strength to stand there, but neither of us took any notice.

After we had had something to eat, Derek sprawled out on the settee and once again fell fast asleep. I sat in the chair and had a little doze but was always conscious of listening for Derek in case he needed anything.

It seemed so strange to be able to look across the room and see Derek actually sitting there in the chair or on the settee. I had never imagined that I would ever get him home so soon, after five weeks in hospital. We were actually a couple again, although I could not help watching his every move and listening at his breathing. Sometimes, when he dozed off he would snore, and then it seemed as though he held his breath. I would say under my breath, *Come on, come on,* and then he would let out a long drawn out breath and I would be so relieved to hear him.

The telephone had rang several times with different family and friends wanting to know how the patient was.

As we sat together in the evening, I told Derek all the events that had happened during the time he spent in hospital, but all he would say was, "Well, I didn't know did I? I thought I had just been asleep."

It was bed time. I wondered what sort of night we would have. He had a bath and climbed into bed. I was really tired but forced myself to keep awake because Derek kept talking. Once the light was out, I thought Derek would soon go to sleep. I must admit I fell fast asleep, but I was woken up by Derek tossing and turning. I asked what was the matter, and he said he had to get up, he was so uncomfortable lying here.

It was just after midnight, so I got a couple of blankets and took them downstairs and then went back up to fetch the pillows. I again made a bed on the three-seater settee for Derek, and I was on the two-seater settee. I knew I would not get a lot of sleep, because I could not stretch my legs out. Then, I had an idea, so I got up and dragged the armchair over to the settee. I positioned the chair so I could lie on the settee with my feet and legs in the arm chair. That was a lot more comfortable.

Derek kept saying, "Go back to bed. I'll be all right down here."

But there was no way I would leave him alone.

Again, we were awake several times during the night. We would have a natter. Then, I would have a little doze, but every time I woke Derek was tossing and turning and kept sighing. I could not wait for daylight to appear, as the darkness made the time go by so slowly.

CHAPTER 38

Wednesday, April 25

I stirred to find Derek was wide awake. It was four thirty in the morning. I got up and made a cup of tea, and we sat talking for ages. Neither of us had had a good night's sleep.

All Derek kept saying was, "Why can't I sleep in a proper bed?"

"Never mind," I said, "It might be because you are sleeping so much during the day."

It was inconvenient that I could not yet use the shower, because it would have been a lot quicker for me, although I would not have been able to give Derek a shower. There was not enough room for a seat inside the cubicle, and he was too weak yet to stand up on his own. I had gotten drenched giving him a shower at the hospital in their wet room, so lord only knows what I would have looked like trying to shower him in a confined space. Gary had ordered the door, but we would have to wait for delivery.

I left Derek sitting on the settee while I went to have a bath. Then, it was his turn to have one.

I got the bed covers all packed away ready for tonight. Derek was all bathed and in clean clothes. Then, we had breakfast and were all ready in case any visitors arrived during the day.

It was a sunny morning, so I asked Derek if he would like to have a walk outside and he said he would. Once outside the door, he had to take hold of my arm. It was a haulage yard, and there was a spacious area for the trucks to turn. We walked round the back and slowly round the perimeter of the yard. Because we were in view of the road, a couple of cars went by and beeped their horns.

Derek said he wanted to go back inside. I thought, apart from the walk from the hospital to the car, that was the longest walk he had had.

During the day, I had an idea that Derek could not sleep because he had been used to a single bed in hospital. We had a single bed in the back bedroom. I wondered if it would work.

Later on during the day, I cleared a space in our bedroom for the single bed. I managed to take the bed to pieces and took it into the bedroom, but I could not put it back together again. I would have to ask one of the boys if they would assemble the bed for me.

During the day, a couple of people called to see Derek, but once they left and we had eaten, Derek dozed off on the settee again. I wished I could go to sleep as quickly as that, but his needs were greater than mine. I covered him up with a blanket and sat in the other room reading, really wanting to go to sleep myself, but always listening for Derek to call me. It was really like when your children are babies, although you think you are asleep, part of you is also awake listening for that cry and or a whimper and you're up to see what's a matter in a flash. It's just the same now.

Gary walked in the door, and I made us all a drink. I explained to Gary what I would like him to do for me, so off he went to put the bed back together. I put clean linen on it while Gary went back downstairs to talk to his dad. I just hoped and prayed that Derek would be able to sleep in there that night.

We sat down during the evening with the television on, and I was trying to find programmes that would interest Derek.

At last, it was bedtime, so Derek climbed into the single bed and I had the double bed. The lights went out, and then it started—every time Derek turned over, the bed creaked. It creaked and creaked as he turned one way and then back again.

I asked if he was OK, and he said, "It's no good. I'll have to get up and go down on the settee, but you can stay here. I don't mind."

"No, I'll come with you," I replied. "If I stay here, I won't be able to sleep."

So, once again it was another night on the settees. Armed with blankets and our pillows, we made our way down stairs. I made us another hot drink before we settled down. This time Derek soon fell asleep, and I soon followed suit.

CHAPTER 39
Thursday, April 26

It was a better night's sleep for both of us. A couple of times we had woken up and spoken to each other, but I think we were both becoming exhausted. I was anyway, but Derek did manage to have a sleep during the day.

We had several visitors call—some who had not seen Derek since his accident but had kept in touch by telephoning once a week. My sister, June, with husband, John, called.

Derek had not been too bad up to then, because when there were two visitors or more sitting in the hospital room they would talk to each other but include Derek in the conversation. However, if it was one to one, it became difficult. Derek could not relate to up-to-date topics or news because he had lost those several weeks since his accident. I would try and join in as much as I could, but I always felt it would be better for Derek to have someone other than me to talk to.

Later in the afternoon, two friends arrived at the same time. Although we had spoken over the telephone, they had not seen Derek, and both were amazed at how well he looked. I made tea, and we sat talking about the latter time Derek spent in Addenbrookes. I said how he had rambled on and on about the truck in the sky, dropping fertilizer. All of a sudden, Derek started it all up again and just kept rambling on and on to the guy who looked puzzled to start with and tried to change the conversation. Derek just kept going back to the same thing for some while. The friends stayed for about three hours. As they left, they said how marvellous I was to keep control of myself and so calm, although the man had had some similar experience in his capacity at his work.

Because Derek had been home for a few days and had not said anything about the episode of the Tony Blair saga, I honestly thought he had forgotten all about it, but one only had to mention a small piece of it and the floodgates opened again. I would make sure to avoid the subject again.

More visitors arrived, but only stayed an hour. Gary came in and had his usual cup of tea, and then it went all quiet.

Derek had a nap on the settee before I cooked some food, which he seemed to be enjoying, but not eating a great amount.

I switched the TV on to watch the news and then switched channels to find a programme Derek might like to watch. By eight thirty, he started to doze, so I kept talking to him to keep him awake so he would have a better chance of sleeping during the night.

After a while, I said we should get ready for bed, but this time I never even bothered to ask where we were going to sleep. I automatically went up to have a wash and then came down with Derek's pillows and cover and made his bed up and then did the same for myself. After making a hot drink, I put the lights out and hoped for the best.

CHAPTER 40
Friday, April 27

Once again, we were awake early, and Derek sat in the armchair watching the birds outside. I tried to go back to sleep again, but it was impossible, so I made a drink and we both sat looking out of the window. There were several birds taking it in turns on the nut feeder. Now and again one would come for a drink in the bird bath and then the favourite trick of the blackbird was to hop along the wall of the fish pond until he got near the waterfall. Then, he would hop on the net that completely covered the pond. As he stood on the net, his weight gradually sank the net just below the water, and he was able to have a bath. Derek really enjoyed watching this. Two or three times a day this occurred with different blackbirds. The two birds had obvious markings on them. One had white markings on both wings and another had a scar over its right eye.

One morning, Derek had looked out of the window to see a heron strutting about on the lawn. It would come to the edge of the fish pond but found the net obstructed his catch and unsuccessfully went away without his breakfast. That was why the net covered the pond. There is a small wood, not so far away from where we live, known as Heron Shore Wood because all the herons gather each evening to roost there.

After I had helped Derek to have a bath and got him dressed, we had breakfast and then various family members and friends started to arrive throughout the morning to see the patient.

I had to take the car to the local garage to have a shock absorber and a spring replaced; I left some friends sitting with Derek while I was away from home.

He did seem to be improving quicker than I expected he would. Was it because we always had family or friends in and out all day? It made a change to see Derek join in their conversations, which I suppose he could now as he listened to the news and was able to talk about other topics. He never watched television or heard the radio while he was in hospital, so he was not up to date with current affairs.

I decided I would cut the lawn, but as usual, the ride-on lawn mower was empty of petrol, so I had to go to the garage to fill up the petrol can. After lunch, Derek was asleep on the settee, so I thought that was the opportunity to cut the grass. After I had been out there a little while, Derek appeared at the window. I went back in the house and opened the French doors and pushed the armchair up against the opening so he was able to sit and watch me.

This evening, we sat in the lounge with the television on but neither of us found anything interesting to watch, so the television was just on. I noticed Derek starting to doze off again, so I suggested we go to bed.

I wanted us to have another go at sleeping in our bed, so we made a drink and went upstairs to get ready for bed and once settled down, I switched the lights out.

CHAPTER 41

Saturday, April 29 and the days that followed

When I stirred and looked at the bedside clock, I could not believe it was nearly eight o'clock. Then, I felt movement next to me and was amazed that Derek was still in bed, let alone asleep. I realized it was the first time since Derek had been out of hospital we had both slept in our bed and not on the settee. What a good sign that was, I hoped he was getting used to the bed once again.

Over the next few days, Derek seemed to be getting stronger and was able to bath and dress himself.

He had come into the bedroom one morning and said, "Do you mind if I try and bathe myself today? I just want to have a go."

I made sure everything was at hand he would need and told him to shout if he felt unsafe. I popped my head in the bathroom a couple of times to make sure he was all right, but he managed fine.

One morning, he even got up first and bought me a cup of tea in bed. I must have been sound asleep, as I never heard him get up. He now was using the toilet himself, unaided.

I would walk outside with him around the garden as he still tended to lean to the right but not as much as he did. I had received a telephone call from the neurology team, and they had made an appointment for May 11 to do a home visit.

I took Derek for a ride in the car to Thetford Forest and another day to Ely. Although we did not get out of the car, it was different scenery for him to look at.

Family and friends had come and gone, and although Derek was getting less confused, on the odd occasion he would suddenly remember the Tony Blair saga.

Everyone was amazed how well he was looking, considering the trauma he had been through; most said that he needed to put some weight back on.

One morning it was lovely and sunny outside, and Derek looked at me and said, "Do you mind if I go for a little walk round the yard on my own? I'll take the mobile with me in case I fall over, and I will be able to call you."

So, off he went. After he had been gone for a few minutes, I crept outside to make sure he was OK but making sure he did not see me. He would always be stroking the dog that lived outside.

It was nerve racking to watch a man once so fit and mobile walk so slowly and unsure of himself, although he was very lucky to be able to do this.

He was eating well and now sleeping much better once he got into the routine.

The day when the neurology team was coming to visit, we sat in the lounge with the back door slightly open and heard the car approach outside.

Derek looked at me and said, "Shall I go and meet them or stay here?"

I answered, "You go and let them him."

A minute or two later, I heard a male voice and then a female one, and Derek walked back into the lounge followed by the couple. I was sitting on the settee behind the door, and they each in turn peered round the door as Derek introduced me to them.

I noticed they looked a bit bewildered, and then I said, "Of course, you have already met Derek."

The guy said, "I can't believe this is the same man I have just read the report on from Addenbrookes hospital. I was expecting another man to be sitting in here. I never dreamt the man who came to the door was the man we have come to see."

The young lady also voiced her opinion as well and said it was a miracle.

After they had gone through records and filled out their report, I made them a drink and we sat chatting. They suggested that we go for walks each day to strengthen Derek's legs, not too far at first, but try and walk a little further each day. I knew I had a pedometer in the drawer, and they said it would be a good idea to monitor his steps and that they would also bring one on their next visit just in case I could not find the one I had. The neurologist arranged for them to call again the following Monday afternoon.

The very next day, was brilliant sunshine again, so I decided to take Derek to a nearby wood. I suppose it was a fifteen-minute drive. There was a rough gravel car park but you could also park off road at various places along the side of the wood, so I decided to pass the turning for the car park and stop in a quiet spot further along.

After sitting a while with the windows down listening to the birds singing and in the distance a large deer run across the roadway and through the trees, I said, "Come on, let's take a little walk."

So, off we started, walking along a dirt track in the clearing of the trees. I suppose we went about 100 yards or so and found some fallen trees to sit on to give Derek a rest. We decided to take a slow walk back to the car.

Once back sitting on the seat, he said, "Oh, my legs ache. I really don't know how I walked back here."

I said, "Let's get you back home."

Driving back along the main road, I asked if he was OK, and he replied that when looking out of the car window his left eye could not keep up with the passing scenery. This was the eye that he kept squinting with when he looked at anyone. I suggested that we mention it to the neurology man on Monday when he called.

The next morning, we walked round the back of the house to a small field we owned next door to the house and noticed a small, off-road motorbike lying in the grass at the corner of the field. The makeshift gate of a wooden pallet tied to the posts with string had been removed and the bike thrown down. As we stood talking, the next door neighbour came out and said she had heard voices out there at one o'clock in the morning. The bike had been obviously stolen, so they said they would notify the police. We had a chat and then left as we were going for our walk.

I parked at the same spot as yesterday, but today I brought two small collapsible stools, very light, to carry with us, so Derek could walk as far as he wanted to and then sit and have a rest. I decided not to walk as far as we had the day before. I suppose we had an hour, and then made our way back home.

As I drove in the yard, I saw the dog was at the full length of his chain lying round the back of the truck shed. I said straight away he was watching someone, so I walked quickly round the back and Derek followed rather more slowly. There stood a police car and a policeman and woman examining the bike, which they had pulled onto the hardcore roadway. I introduced myself and explained how we found it. By this time, Derek had walked round and joined us. The officers hands were dirty from where they had pulled the bike from the field, so I went in and fetched some baby wipes.

While they were cleaning themselves up, the lady police officer said to me, "We have met before haven't we?"

After a couple of seconds, I remembered she was the officer who have driven me to the hospital on the day of Derek's accident.

She asked a few questions and said, "I can't believe this is the same man. I have been standing here looking at him and thinking this cannot be the man that was lying on the road in a pool of blood. When I first saw you walk over to us, I dare not ask any questions, as I thought that man had not survived that fall. Then, I thought it must have been a brother or your son that had had the fall."

Then, the policeman said, "It's unbelievable that anyone could possibly recover as quickly as that, as there was a lot of red wine about [blood]."

We explained that Derek had not cut his head open as we all thought at the time, and they could not believe it. We stood chatting for some time. They said they had telephoned the hospital the next morning after the accident and was told the patient had been taken to Addenbrookes, but after that they had been unable enquire. The police lady said it was lovely to actually meet Derek, and she would be able to tell the other officers that were on the scene how well Derek had recovered. They wheeled the bike to the gate and waited for a police van to arrive to remove it.

If the weather was wet or cold, I would find a different route to drive Derek, all along the country roads, mainly to the places where Derek used to do most of his agricultural contracting. We would talk about different farmers and their ways of wanting work done. This I know he enjoyed, and he was able to remember things that happened years ago.

CHAPTER 42
Monday, May 14

Bob, the neurologist, was not coming until that afternoon, so off we went on another walk. It was at the same woods, but we parked in the car park and walked a different route. Derek seemed to be able to walk a little further now and said his legs did not ache so much.

After we got back home and had had something to eat and drink, we waited for Bob to call. (Derek called him the "Shrink," as he was not very good at remembering names.)

When Bob appeared, he sat for a while asking how the walking was going and ask if we could record how many steps Derek did each day and supplied a rather up-market pedometer.

I also mentioned to him about Derek's left eye not being able to focus on the passing scenery, and he said it would take a little time to repair itself after the head injury he received, but if, as time went on it did not improve then he would have to arrange to see an eye specialist.

He then asked if they could sit at the dining room table as he wanted to do some tests with Derek.

Once at the table, Derek was given a sheet of A4 paper with perhaps six boxes with a different unfinished drawing in each box. Bob asked Derek to complete each picture. I can remember the first drawing was of a sitting room with a fireplace with one half of a clock face standing on a mantel piece and only half the figures on it. Derek had to complete the clock face, add the numbers inside it, and put the hands the exact time as it was at that moment. I cannot remember what the other pictures consisted of as I went to the other end of the room to the kitchen to make a cup of tea.

Once Derek completed that task, next Bob produced a pack of postcard-sized cards with drawings on them and placed them on the table. Bob then told a story by placing the cards in order of the story. For example, a drawing of some fruit was on one card, a parcel ready to be posted, and a newsagent's kiosk. Bob placed the cards on the table as the story. For example, Mr Smith went into town as he wanted to post a parcel. From there he went into the newsagent's to buy a newspaper and some sweets. He crossed the road at the zebra crossing and went into the fruit shop to buy apples, pears, plums, and so on. There were different cards to connect with a different story each time.

Derek was all right with the first story, as it was a short one, but after that, he could not remember what order things should have been in. At the end of the tests, Derek scored nine out of sixteen.

Derek was told he could potter about in the workshop but not to use any electrical equipment such as drills. As we walked outside, the neurologist ask me to keep an eye on Derek. Let him go and mess about in the workshop, but don't leave him too long before you make sure he is all right. He also said it would not hurt to make an appointment with his GP so he could see how Derek was progressing now he was at home. He made arrangements to call again on Thursday the seventeenth. That very next morning I rang the GP's surgery and made the appointment for next week.

CHAPTER 43
Working with Annie

Derek was now sleeping less during the day and walking about more, rather than sitting in the house dozing.

Derek owned a classic car, a Triumph Herald 13/60 convertible that I bought for him for our twenty-fifth wedding anniversary. For years, he had kept saying that "one of these days" he was going to get himself a Triumph convertible, but he never did. However, when I was working, I managed to save up to get him one. He loved tinkering about with it. You can almost stand inside the engine compartment and see what's what—not like today's modern computerised car that you have to go to a garage to have it plugged into a computer. Then, the screen reads out what's wrong with it.

He named the car Annie, short for Anniversary. The ride-on lawn mower is called Arnie, and the wood burner in the shed is Bertha, so we could call out, "Just going to make Bertha up" instead of making the boiler up or "Get Arnie out, will you?" Well, we knew as a family what each other was talking about.

Before his accident, Derek removed the differential and drive shafts to replace a seal that was worn on the Triumph and never had time to put it all back together again. It was in bits in the garage.

Anyway, Stuart was on holiday from work, and he and his dad had discussed how to put back the differential and drive shafts. Stuart agreed to have a go at it, if his dad would give out instructions as what to do, I think it involved some heavy lifting, and Derek was not strong enough to do it yet. So, with a chair in the garage, Derek sat giving orders as what to do, and both were enjoying it. I think it took about three days to complete the task, but Stuart did not always arrive to start work until nearly lunch time each day.

We would go for our usual walks in the morning, and Derek was walking further each day but it depended on the weather. Sometimes, if it was chilly or wet, we would just sit in the car with the windows open listening to the birds singing. There would always be a robin appear and sit in a bush right next to the car and start singing his little song or a woodpecker in the distance knocking on the side of a tree with its beak. The blackbirds and jays would be turning the fallen leaves over at the base of the trees, or we would see a squirrel scamper by. Derek did so love the wildlife—well, we both do.

We sat talking and decided we would listen to the weather forecast. If it talked of being a bright, sunny morning, we would come here early when there was not so many people about walking their dogs and see what wildlife we would discover then. We were always awake early, and it would be a bit of a challenge for us.

On Thursday, the neurology team was coming again in the morning, so walking would have to wait until later. It was two young ladies who came and basically asked Derek lots of questions. They looked at his hand, said it was still badly swollen, and gave him some exercises to do, like squeezing a soft tennis ball and making a fist by opening and closing his fingers, to try and reduce the swelling. While one of them was talking to Derek, I asked the other one some questions. I said that he had never had a seizure, and I was gob smacked when she said he still could have one and gave me instructions on how to cope if he did. They did not stop too long and said they would be back in a week's time.

It was almost two months since the accident and I always thought how lucky Derek was to get away without too many problems, but after knowing he could have a seizure I began to get paranoid. Derek would make an unusual noise, and I would immediately ask if he was OK. He usually replied that he had only hiccupped or made a noise when he yawned.

At night in bed, he would fall asleep straight away, and I would lay there and listen to him snoring. He would inhale, and I keep saying, "Come on, come on, breathe out." It seemed ages before he exhaled again, and if I thought it was too long I would nudge him and make him wake up. He would ask what was the matter, and I would reply, "Oh nothing." I never did say why I had woken him up.

One day, Derek walked 9,972 steps, the highest yet. We had walked the longest route through the woods, and then in the afternoon, I said I was going to take the dog along the footpath near our house and Derek said he would come with me.

We went to the surgery to keep Derek's appointment. The GP was also amazed at how well Derek had recovered from his traumatic head injury. The doctor advised me to notify the Driver and Vehicle Licensing Agency to voluntarily surrender his driving license. It would be at least another four months before he could reapply for it again. According to the type of injury and recovery period, it was usually six months or more after release from hospital.

I said to Derek, "Never mind mate, my taxi service is not that expensive and I'm on call 24/7."

I tried to make a laugh of it but understood how he must feel well enough in mind to be able to drive, but as I said to him, if he was not fit enough and he knocked over a child or hit another car and killed someone, he would feel a hell of a lot worse. So he had to come to terms with it.

He gave a sigh and said, "I suppose you're right, but you don't know what it's like after having been able to just jump in the car and go where you want, without having to rely on someone else all the time. But if that's what it's got to be, then I shall just have to live with it."

A few days later, around 2.30 a.m., the telephone rang. It was a neighbour to ask if I could go over there, his elderly mother was feeling poorly. When I arrived, we decided to call an ambulance. Once she was put in the ambulance I told the son that we would follow the ambulance to the hospital in the car. He asked me if I would mind going on my own, as he did not like sitting around in hospitals. The paramedic's told me there was no rush and to drive there when I was ready.

When I got back home, Derek was already dressed and had made me a cup of tea. I explained what was going to happen, and he said that he would come with me. I told him that was not necessary, but he said, "You were always there for me, and now it's my turn to be there for you."

We answered a mountain of questions relating to the lady, as I had known them for about twelve years and knew their life history. We stayed with her until 6.00 a.m., and then we left her as she was wheeled into the assessment ward. Once home, we had a drink and then went to bed to snatch a couple of hours' sleep.

After the doctors had done various tests on her, they said they could not find anything seriously wrong with her and she was allowed home later that day.

By the end of the week, Derek had raised his walking steps to 12,313 one day by walking the longest route through the woods. Instead of turning right to go back toward the car, we turned left, following the track at the side of the wood and then took another route through the trees and made our way back toward the car from a different route. The sun was shining fairly warm, and it just felt really good to be able to be out and enjoy the day.

One morning, we did actually leave the house 5.45a.m. to go to the woods. We sat very still and quiet for about an hour before we decided to go for a walk, and to our surprise, we never saw any wildlife at all, not even a dog with its master; we could only hear the birds singing high above in the tree tops, but it was a glorious morning and well worth getting up early.

The strange thing was that Derek never ever wanted to sit and talk about his accident. I would tell him about the ward, nurses, visitors, etc. and all he kept saying was, "I don't know do I?" As far as I'm concerned, it was that I went to sleep and woke up the next morning."

So, five weeks of his life did not exist. He never asked any questions, the only thing that seemed to be imprinted in his brain was the blackbird in the garden at Addenbrookes.

CHAPTER 44
The Mobile Phone and the Hiding

We would go for the usual walk, and after we got home Derek would tinker about in the workshop. As advised, I found any excuse to wander over there to see if he was all right. I walked over there to hear a voice coming from inside the workshop. For a moment, I hesitated before I walked in as I thought he had one of his mates or neighbours in there with him. Then it went quiet, so I walked in, and Derek was on his own.

I said in a surprised voice, "Oh, I thought you had someone in here with you."

Derek replied, "No, I was just singing."

I took no notice of his reply, but I had never heard him hum or sing to himself before. I just accepted his answer.

Another day, he had been outside for a while, and yet again I was desperate to know if he was OK. I had seen his mobile on the unit in the kitchen and thought, *Shall I take it out to him?* I decided not to, but as I walked across the yard, Derek was somewhere behind the large truck shed over in the yard talking. Sometimes, the neighbour would come through the back way if he knew Derek was about outside and have a chat to him. I really felt guilty snooping on him, but I was only doing what I was asked to do and check on him. I went back inside, but I still heard him talking to someone.

After a while, he came back in, and I said casually, "Anyone about?"

He said, "No, I just went for a walk round the back to have a look about."

I asked if any of the neighbours had seen him outside and come round.

"No. I just had a wander about and then went to have a look at the rain gauge to see how much rain fell overnight."

This type of thing went on for days. Sometimes, his mobile would ring, and he would take it outside to talk as the signal was never very good inside the house. Through the kitchen window, I could see him walk back and forth across the yard while on the phone.

I smiled. Why do men have to keep walking around when they are using the mobile? I have seen many a man do this when they have been at the house—the window cleaner, mechanic, tyre-repair man, and the diesel-delivery guy.

Well, at least Derek was adding to his pedometer. Then, he came in and said it was one of the men from the factory calling to see how he was progressing.

Today, our son Stuart called to do a few odd jobs for us and was outside talking with his Dad, after a while he came in and said, "Oh, Mum. I stood talking to Dad, and he couldn't wait to get rid of me. He asked me to go and fetch something, and as soon as I left, he stood leaning against the cab of his truck on his bloody mobile phone."

"No he wasn't," I replied.

"Yes, he was Mum. I heard him talking the minute I walked away. He was just finding excuses for me to leave him alone and in the middle of a conversation at that."

I said, "No, I don't think he was, Stuart."

He said, "Mum, I heard him talking, and his hand was up against his ear."

The Three Birds

I pointed to Derek's mobile phone lying on the kitchen unit and explained to Stu that this had happened several times before.

Over the next couple of weeks, the same thing happened, time after time. I would walk outside, and Derek would have his hand up against his ear talking away, but there would be nothing in his hand. His mobile would very often be left in the house or if he had taken it with him, it would still be in his pocket.

I told Stuart that the mobile problem still happened frequently, and he said, "Mum, you ought to have a word with someone about."

I said I would call the neurologist first thing in the morning.

The next morning, I waited until Derek was in full conversation with a friend who had called. I made them a drink and went upstairs to telephone Bob the neurologist from our bedroom. I rang the hospital, and as luck should have it, Bob had not left the office to do his house calls. I explained the situation, and he told me not to worry too much about it. He said that Derek really thought in his mind he was actually having a conversation with someone. He could have been on his mobile just before his fall, and that was why he was continually using a make-believe mobile.

His brain had to slowly repair itself. It was like having a chain with some broken links, and you cannot repair them all at the same time. If the brain has been damaged, it has to find another way round to link up with the unbroken chain. It could take up to two years before his brain sorted itself out.

Think of it as a stream or river—if it becomes blocked, the water eventually finds another route.

I have got an appointment to see him and we will go from there. He said don't worry too much about it now.

As time went by, the talking on the imaginary mobile phone did finally cease.

The other strange thing was that he would run and hide when he heard footsteps approaching him. I noticed this I went to the supermarket and left Derek for the first time at home alone since the accident. Other times that I had gone out, I always made sure that someone was there with him. One night, I went with my daughter-in-law at eight o'clock at night to do the weekly shopping, while Stuart sat with his dad. This was most unheard for me, as it was usually early in the morning when I went shopping.

He was messing about over the shed, so I walked over to him and said I would be leaving in about five minutes.

He said, "Don't worry, I'm not going to do anything silly or go anywhere."

I suppose I would leave him alone for about an hour and a quarter by the time I left the house, drove to the supermarket, got the shopping, and drove back again. I drove the car to the edge of the road and happened to glance in the rear-view mirror and saw Derek peeping at me from behind the passenger side of his truck. I thought he was just watching me drive away.

On my return, I drove into the yard, and on the far side of the parked truck under the gap of the trailer, I saw a pair of rigger boots quickly making their way to the back of the truck shed. I parked the car and walked over to where Derek had run to, to see if he was OK.

He stood at the back of the trailer, messing about with the rear lights. I asked if he had been OK.

He said, "Yes, just been buggering about."

After then, every time he was outside and heard a car or footsteps on the gravel, he would run into the shed or round the back of the yard and hide.

Stuart came to see him every day, if his shift pattern would allow, and he came to me and said, "Mum, two or three times when I've come here Dad has been running away and disappearing into the back of the truck shed, and yesterday I was walking over to the workshop when I saw his feet from the other side of the truck, running to the back of it. I called out to him, but he would not answer. I walked toward him, shouting to him, and he said he never heard me call."

Luck should have it, I did not have to discuss this matter in front of Derek. We were speaking one day to Bob, when Derek's mobile rang. It was a guy from the hemp factory where Derek hauled the bales too on behalf of the farmers calling to have a chat with Derek. So, while Derek was talking to him, I was able to tell Bob about this problem. I explained that at the time of the accident, when Derek was lying on the road and the paramedics were working on him, all of a sudden he started to move his feet and legs as though trying to get up and run. I knelt down and held his feet together to stop him fighting against them.

Bob said that Derek was probably conscious of someone pinning him down, and he was trying to get up and run away. Now, when he hears a vehicle or someone talking, he might well think someone is coming to take him away again, so if he hides, they can't take him. In time, he would overcome this problem

Again it did pass in time. It did make me more wary. I tended to watch out more and more to make sure Derek was safe at all times.

CHAPTER 45

Test, Scans, and Appointments

When Bob called again and said he had a couple of tests for Derek to do.

We sat at the dining room table, and Bob took out a silver case about the size of a brief case. When it was fully opened, it lay flat like an open book. One side contained all different-sized, coloured, round wooden pegs set in their own slots. Of course, the lid of the case was empty except for the indentations where the wooden pegs fitted when the lid was closed.

Bob said, "I would like you to put all the pegs from this side, in the same colour and size as they are there, and put them in the other side (the lid), and I'm going to time you just to see how long it will take you."

Derek closed the case up, turned it over, and put it back down with the lid side on the table. He opened it, and—hey presto—all the pegs were in the lid side as it should have ended up.

Derek looked at Bob and said, "There you are. All done."

It had taken Derek less than five seconds for him to do that.

Bob smiled and said, "I'm sorry, but that's not allowed, you have to pick them up and put them in the empty side one at a time."

Derek replied, "You never said that. You just said they had to be moved from one side to the other, and that's what I've done."

Case closed. Bob could not argue with that.

The next test is going to be hard to explain. Bob told Derek that he was going to make a wire coat hanger. He pulled out a wooden base with pins set around the base with which you could form a full-size coat hanger, using a bending tool provided. He then handed Derek the piece of wire with a diagram to make the coat hanger.

The wire had to be bent round the pins using the bending tool; on each bend two of the pins were set out wider than the rest. Derek used those to retain the wire from bending outwards. He was told that internal bend force had to have an external stopping force of equivalent strength to be able to bend the wire.

Derek finished the task in hand, laughed, and said, "One coat hanger."

Then, he handed it to Bob for inspection.

Bob pointed out that he had put the wire on the wrong side of the pins and of course did not follow the diagram, so he once again lost points.

On his next visit, Bob came with another experiment for Derek.

Out of Bob's magical bag he produced four steel, flat, square plates, with four threaded studs with spacers on each corner. The plates and studs were different sizes and Bob explained to Derek that he was to build a pyramid and once again produced a diagram, which Derek put to one side straight away.

Derek started using the largest plate first and then inserted each plate in turn, because he said it was easier to put the studs on each thread on top, instead of underneath. On reaching the top of the finished pyramid, he turned it the right way up, pleased it was complete.

But the smile soon disappeared when Bob said, "You never followed the diagram. You should have started with the smallest first. So I'll have to take some points off for that."

A friend had called earlier and said to Derek, "Well, mate, you won't be doing a show this December will you?"

Derek quickly answered, "Oh, yes I will. I'm getting better. Those children who we raise money for are not."

I told Bob about this, and he asked if we had a video or DVD he could take home to watch and return it the next time he called. I found the DVD of the March show, and Bob took it away with him.

On his next visit, he produced from his magical bag four different wooden structures. Different-sized wooden pieces were glued onto a flat wooden base. These wooden pieces stood up to make a scene—for instance a tower, a bridge, oblong and triangle shapes, etc. Derek was given four bases and a pile of wooden shapes and had to arrange these shapes in the same order as those already glued on. Three seemed easy for Derek to copy, but the fourth one was a very busy scene, as the wooden pieces were at all different angles, although Derek did achieve this in the end, it took a little longer for him to fathom out.

Bob had made a note of all the tests that had been done so he could make a report on Derek's progress.

Then Bob said, "I don't think there is anything more I can do for you. I watched the DVD, and there is a lot of work to be done if you intend performing this December show. It's nearly the end of June now, so I have arranged for the physiotherapist to come along and give you some exercises to build the muscles up in your arms and legs. At the moment, you are still slightly leaning to one side, and there is no way you can perform all those moves that you did on that DVD."

So, the physiotherapist made two or three visits, teaching Derek various exercises. One used a dining room chair, which I had to sit on to stop it from falling over. Derek stood behind, holding the back of the chair. Then, he had to keep bending his knees, gradually getting lower and lower each time. For another, he had to lie down on the floor with me holding his feet to stop them from raising up. Then, with his arms folded across his chest, he had to gradually pull himself up. He would have to do these exercises five times each for five days, then ten times a day for five days, and so on.

So either before our walk or after we got back, Derek religiously did these exercises every day, as he was so determined he was going to be fit for that December charity concert.

In September 2007, Derek had to report back to Addenbrookes Traumatic Brain Injury Clinic and to the Wolfson Brain Imaging Centre for another scan and computerized memory tests. This was all part of the research programme.

The first appointment was for the MRI scan. To reach this unit, we had to walk through the main hospital, then through the back doors to outside, walk across the so-familiar garden.

Derek said straight away, "This is where that female blackbird was feeding, picking up pieces of food and flying off and then coming back again."

"Oh, good, you remembered," I said.

Then there was a building on our left. We had to press a button and wait for a member of staff to let us in. In the corner on the left was a small reception desk. Once Derek had given his details, we were asked to sit in a small waiting room. While waiting, we were both given a questionnaire to fill in regarding Derek's health, abilities or disabilities, and in general his reactions since he had left hospital.

A nurse then came to take Derek to have his scan. He was probably gone twenty minutes. Then, he returned with another member of staff with his notes, who asked us to follow her.

We then had to go back through the garden into the main hospital and back to corridor in front of the main hall. We approached it from a different direction. At this point, if Derek had still been in the ward, I would have turned right, but this day he was by my side and we turned left, walking nearly to the end of the long corridor, turning right into a lift to take us to the upper floor, through double doors, and into a small waiting area.

We were given a cup of tea and some sandwiches. Thirty minutes later, a young lady we had met before came through and asked us to go into a small room where stood a desk with a large computer on it, two chairs in front of the desk, and one chair against the back wall. Derek sat on the chair directly in front of the desk, and the lady moved the other chair slightly away from the desk. I sat on the chair at the back, but because the room was small I was not sitting that far away from Derek.

Derek sat in front. The lady explained that when he was ready to start he had to press a button and then the screen went into action. It was all touch-screen tests.

Firstly, I can remember two boxes appeared. One box turned white, the other box turned red, and then screen went blank. The boxes reappeared, both white again. Derek had to remember which box had been the red one and touch that box on the screen, which was easy to start with. Then, it gradually went to three boxes, then four, then five, then six. Each time only one of the boxes turned red, and each time the boxes where jumbled up, but as it got more boxes the less time you had to choose the red box.

The next programme was similar, but this time, when two boxes appeared, one had a picture of a hand saw in it and the other one a rabbit for instance. (It was just the saw that stuck in my mind.) Then, the boxes closed, and a picture appeared at the top of the screen, like the hand saw. He had to touch the box on the screen that he thought the hand saw was in. Again, by the end of the test, there were nine boxes, opening up and then closing, and of course nine different pictures, so the tests got harder. It was all about his concentration ability.

Another test I seem to remember was adding up and subtracting of figures, but as I am writing this from memory, once again it has failed me.

For the last test, Derek had to place bets in a box at the top, right-hand side of the screen. He had a certain amount of money to place a bet with, and he could use as little or as much money as he wanted.

Now since Derek was not a betting man, I thought he would find this more difficult than the other tests, but he achieved a higher score on this test than on any of the others.

There were three rows of cubes going from left to right across the screen, one row red, one white, and one blue. Derek had to choose a colour and bet the amount of money he wanted to gamble. Some cubes were a higher risk than others. Depending on how far each line crossed the screen, it was at a higher percentage of risk. This test was to find out if Derek could work out the percentage, subtract, and add. For example, if the red line of cubes went across the screen to 70 per cent, that meant you could bet 30 per cent of whatever money you had in your box.

Once the tests were finished, Derek and I made our way back through the gardens but this time turning right into a building, then taking the lift to the upper floor, as he had an appointment in the Traumatic Brain Injury Clinic.

It was a small waiting area with perhaps a dozen chairs in it, and more chairs lined the corridor each side. It was packed with patients of all ages waiting to see a doctor.

We had to stand for a while until two chairs became available. It seemed as though when one patient had been dismissed by the doctor, two more joined the queue for their appointments.

It was finally Derek's turn. The young doctor did not seem a familiar face to me, as I had not seen him on the ward. We were asked to sit down while he studied Derek's notes. He asked a few questions and then said come back to the clinic in a year's time, an appointment will be sent out to you.

Very few words were spoken, until we got out side in the fresh air, and all Derek said was, "Well that's that then. Another year to wait."

I asked Derek if he would like to go to the critical-care ward to see if any of the nurses were still working on that ward when he was in there. He replied, "If you like."

We made our way to the NCCU, and all Derek kept saying was that nothing seemed familiar to him. I pushed the buzzer to notify that someone was waiting to gain entry onto the ward. Once the buzzer sounded, a doctor or nurse would look at one of the TV monitors—one was situated behind the reception desk and another one on the wall above the nurse's desk on the ward—someone would then release door lock mechanisms so we could walk in.

Once at the reception desk, I explained to the young lady why we were there and asked if Nick, the male nurse who helped to look after Derek, was on duty. She telephoned through to the ward, and said Nick was not on duty today but someone would be along shortly to show Derek around the unit.

By this time my tummy was in knots and I really did feel sick, as all the memories came flooding back when I had made this journey so many times, and although Derek was beside me this time, it did not make it any more pleasant.

The door opened, and a young nurse smiled and asked us to follow her through the doors. Although she was speaking I felt numb and did not really know what she was talking about. I saw the patients lying there, as once Derek had, with the monitors flashing and bleeping and with tubes in every orifice possible. As we walked through the ward, we neared the bed Derek had been in, although we did not approach the bed as there was a patient occupying it. The nurse stopped, looked at Derek, and said this is the bed you were in, Number 11. A young girl possibly about ten years old was laying there with a head cage on. At first, she had been staring up at the ceiling; then without moving her head, her eyes moved to where we were standing.

Derek then asked the nurse if he could go over and speak to the girl.

Once given permission, he walked to the bottom of the bed and said, "Hello. You'll be fine, as this is a lucky bed. A few weeks ago, I was laying there and now look at me."

The girl smiled, and Derek walked back to where we were standing.

I was disappointed not to have recognized any of the nurses on duty today, but I think they have to work on different wards to get the experience needed.

We walked to the far end of the ward, and then I pointed out to Derek the other area he was moved to, which was the High Dependency Unit.

A male voice then said, "Hello. Good to see you. How are you doing?"

The speaker shook Derek's hand. He was another male nurse who had worked on the ward at the time Derek was in there, but I only spoke to him four or five times, so he was not really that familiar to me.

Once through the swing doors, past some small rooms to our left, where the visitors wore aprons and masks, it was back through another set of swing doors and back to the reception desk. We both thanked the nurse and walked out back to the main corridor.

My legs were like jelly, and I was as dry as a fish, so once we reached the main area, I headed straight for the cafeteria and found a table. I walked over to the familiar counter where I knew I could buy some chips and then got us both a cup of tea.

Then Derek said, "I didn't know this place existed. How did you know where to go to buy these?"

I replied, "Oh, Derek, other than sitting by your bed, this is the only other place to come to. You've been in here several times before."

I then went on to the different times we had pushed him here in his chair, but he said, "I can't remember this place at all."

All the way home, Derek kept repeating, "Why can't I remember the hospital and yet I can remember the blackbird?"

CHAPTER 46
Air Ambulance Visit

Although Derek was recovering more as each week passed, his mood did not. He did not like mooching around the house, and he had nothing outside to occupy his mind.

I encouraged him do the exercises that the physiotherapist had shown him, and he did them without making any fuss.

Once he had cut the hawthorne and conifer hedge, it did not need cutting anymore, as it was late autumn. Each week, he had cut the grass on the ride-on mower, but now that did not need cutting again until spring time. We would go for our usual walks, but he was so unsettled and really seemed tetchy when I asked him a question, his reply would be so sharp.

He had been such an active person by working; he just could not adjust to being around the house.

I had driven him to places far and wide and friends called to chat to him, but nothing seemed to help. He had loved messing around with the grandchildren, but he had even lost interest in doing that.

In late October, without Derek knowing, I rang the East Anglian Air Ambulance headquarters at Norwich to ask if it would be possible to bring Derek along to see the Air Ambulance helicopter that had taken him to hospital on the day of the accident. The young lady was very helpful and said if I could give her the date of the accident and where it happened, she would try and organize the doctor, paramedic, and pilot to be there as well. So, a date was arranged for the next week, a late afternoon visit as the helicopter did not fly after dark, so it was usually in the hangar around 4.30 p.m.

Our youngest son, Stuart, and his wife were in on the surprise. I asked Gary if he would like to come along as well, but he was unable to come as he had other plans for that evening.

On the day before we were due to go, I had to find an excuse why we should be going to Norwich. That evening, Stuart and Caroline came in, and we started talking about kitchens and bathrooms, as we needed a new kitchen.

Stuart said, "We have the day off tomorrow. Let's go and have a look round at some."

In the back of Stuart's car I had hidden a bag containing tins of sweets and biscuits for the staff to nibble at throughout the day as a very small token of thanks for the East Anglian Air Ambulance headquarters, as you could not give to just one person. It was a joint effort. Someone had to take the call and then relay directions to the scene. And, of course, I had that all important thank-you card.

Derek was not one for shopping at all and had a little moan about going. He said would rather stay at home, but Stuart can be very persuasive at times and said it would be something different; neither of us mentioned that we were heading to Norwich.

It was a cold, sunny day, and we were all ready. I had butterflies in my tummy, as it bought back all the memories again, but I wanted Derek to see how he was taken to hospital and looked after. But mostly I wanted for him to realize how serious his injury had been and try and help him understand why he could not just jump back in his truck again so soon after the accident. We got into Stuart's car and set off, and then Derek asked where we were going.

We had managed to drive a few miles away from our village, when I said, "I never told you before, because you would have only moaned, but we are going to Norwich."

Stuart butted in and said there was a lovely kitchen and bathroom showroom just on the outskirts of Norwich. He did not know this until he had looked on the internet the night before and discovered a showroom only a few hundred yards from the turning to Norwich airport where the helicopter was kept overnight.

"Bloody hell!" Derek said, "All the bathrooms and kitchens places there are around here, and we've got to go all the way to Norwich."

Stuart said, "Yes, Dad, but there isn't one round here like that one in Norwich."

We were almost there and my heart was beating ninety to the dozen, but it was only three thirty and our appointment was not until four o'clock. As we drove along the road, Stuart suddenly turned into a car-sales forecourt.

He said, "Look at these, Dad. You are always on about a CAT [Jaguar]. Let's have a look at these."

We all got out of the car to wander about, but the wind was so cold and I was not really interested in cars, so I decided to get back in our car in the warm. It was obvious Stuart was stalling for time.

We had hardly got back on the road when Stuart pointed out the kitchen and bathroom showroom.

He said, "Oh, I've missed the turning. I'll turn round and go back."

He indicated a right turn, which was signposted "Norwich Airport." He followed the road round, and on the right of us was the security fence with aircraft moving along the runway. We all made different remarks about going on holiday, forgot our passports, etc. Then, Stuart parked the car, and we all clambered out.

"Oh, well," Derek said, "I suppose I'd better come in with you."

I replied, "Yes, you had better. Look where we are."

I pointed to the sign above the door that read EAST ANGLIAN AIR AMBULANCE HEADQUARTERS.

For the first time that day, Derek was speechless. Stuart pushed the doorbell as requested, and we waited for someone to come to let us in.

We entered the building and then climbed a flight of stairs, through a door, and into the main office of the ambulance service. We were then introduced to two members of staff sitting at their desks, answering non-medical calls. We found out minutes later, they worked on the charity side of the operations team.

We stood listening to head of operations, as he was explaining how this side of the Air Ambulance worked, when the door opened and in walked the doctor that worked on Derek at the scene, along with the helicopter pilot. We all introduced ourselves, and the doctor told Derek he looked a lot better than he did when he last saw him.

Derek gave them the thank-you card and tins of sweets and biscuits. It seemed such a trivial thing to be handing them when they saved your life, but at least it was something they could all share.

They asked if we were ready to go downstairs to where the helicopter flew back to base every night. We followed the doctor downstairs, through a door, and then had to walk across a large hanger through another door to the outside of the building. There was activity all around us, and we had to walk close to the building and make sure we kept inside the yellow line for safety reasons. The doctor stopped and slide back a large door into another hanger and there stood the helicopter, ANGLIA 1.

Stuart and Caroline were talking and had walked ahead with the doctor and pilot. I stood at the side of Derek, and then I spoke to him and there came no reply. I walked in front of him, and at that moment I saw tears running down his cheeks and his mouth was quivering.

I went up to him and put my arms around him. He laid his head on my shoulder and mumbled something I could not understand and started to sob. It went through my mind, had I done the right thing by bringing him here or was it too much for him? I stepped back and asked if he would rather go back outside, but there was no reply.

After what seemed like several minutes Derek finally uttered, "I shall be OK."

Wiping the tears away, he said, "It was just the sight of the helicopter that helped save my life, and here I am lucky enough to be alive to be able to come back and look at it from the other side."

We slowly walked to the side of the others. Stuart got Derek to stand between the doctor and the pilot, and he took some photographs. The pilot excused himself as he had to make his way home. The doctor asked Derek if he would like to sit in the seat in the back of the helicopter, near to where the stretcher would have been. He then explained in detail all the instruments, switches, levers, and how they used them while flying to the hospital. In turn, we were asking questions. Derek was still sitting in the seat. Stuart and Caroline had wandered off to look round the front, while I stood next to the doctor, listening to him explaining different things when we noticed Derek became emotional again. The doctor stood facing Derek but continued talking to me, but at the same time he put a hand on Derek's shoulder to comfort him. At that point, I walked away, because it was just as emotional for me.

Derek seemed to sit inside the back of the helicopter for some time; I joined Stuart and Caroline and left Derek still sitting inside the helicopter. The reality of what had happened showed there on Derek's face.

The Three Birds

Sitting in Air Ambulance

After a while we all got back together again, we were shown the police helicopter, one that was used in a James Bond film. There was also another small aircraft standing there, along with another Air Ambulance. We heard several interesting stories connected with each helicopter, and then we made our way back upstairs. This time, we went into the room where the paramedics and crew sat and made their reports. Maps were on the wall and a board with flight details on. A tall guy sat at the desk, and he was introduced to us as another paramedic. Derek sat on a chair while Stuart, Caroline, and I sat on a settee. Again, the conversation went back to the day of the accident. They could both recall when the call came through and the weather conditions. They remembered the field they had landed in and the bonfire with the rubbish blowing about caused by the rotor blades. They explained to us how serious Derek had been and how they never thought they would ever see him looking so well. They carried on to explain all the things that happen when a call comes through.

Sometime after that, I noticed the clock on the wall read six fifteen. I knew these guys had been working and had still to travel home, so I suggested it was about time we made our way back home. We thanked them for their hospitality, and they gave us a goody bag to take with us.

Derek repeatedly kept saying "thank you" to the two guys while shaking their hand, each in turn. The doctor, who had escorted us round, said it was our job and the only thank you they needed, was to see Derek walk through that door and say hello, because to them that meant they won.

On the way back home, we had decided to stop for fish and chips and sat in the car to eat them, but all Derek kept on about was how he walked into that hanger and thought he was just going to see where the helicopter was sometimes stationed and it blew him away to actually see it stand there.

It was the talking point with Derek many days after that visit, and I was really happy that I had arranged for him to meet the guys and see where he had been in a helicopter journey he knew nothing about.

CHAPTER 47

Elvis Concert

A week before the show, I rang the local paper to ask if they now wanted to produce a story on Derek's accident and to promote the forthcoming Elvis Concert. After giving them a story, we made an appointment for their photographer to come and take some pictures later that day. The story would then be in the paper at the end of the week

On Friday morning, I made my way to the shop in the next village, can you imagine the shock I received when I drew in the car park and the billboard in very large letters read "ELVIS IS BACK FROM THE DEAD." I had to sit in the car for a few minutes, as I did not know whether I was going to cry or not. After composing myself, I went inside the shop and lifted the local paper from the stand. There it was, a front page story, with the same words in bold letters as on the billboard.

During the day, different ones telephoned to say they had seen the posters outside the shops in villages where they lived and had made them go cold or made them think of what might have been.

We had been rehearsing every week ready for the show, as I am also one of the backing singers. Derek was asked a hundred times if he was all right, and his reply remained the same: "Yes, I'm fine."

On the day of the concert, we made our way to the seaside town of Hunstanton to the venue. I must admit I had butterflies in my tummy and again my thoughts were on how Derek was going to get on during the show.

On arrival, we were kept busy by making sure everything was going to plan. The audience had started to queue outside the main doors, and as I walked through the door to make sure the lady selling tickets had everything she needed, I was approached by a lady who lives in our village. She was carrying a book like a photograph album. She asked if I would like to be the first to write on the inside page. On the front of the book was a photograph of Derek in his Elvis suit from a previous show, and the lady was going to go round every member of the audience and Elvis team to get them to write a message for Derek on the blank pages inside.

I took the book and opened it at the first page and with the pen I went to write, but I started to cry and had to leave the book and go back inside the venue. Once I regained myself, I went back outside to talk to different members of the audience. Some had been to every show and so had become our friends. Then, comments started flying around: are you sure Derek will be OK? you know those flashing lights could start a seizure. What if he slips on stage? There are a lot of strenuous movements he'll be doing. And it went on and on.

I just walked off and headed for the darkness of the other smaller but empty clubroom. Someone must have reported back to one of the Elvis team that I was upset, and the more people came in asking if I was OK, the more the tears came.

I just wanted Derek to come to give me a cuddle and reassure me everything was going to be all right, but he did not appear.

But his mate, Mike, came into the room and said, "We did not want Derek to know you were crying or why, as we did not want him to get upset at what people had been saying as well, but he is absolutely fine."

After a chat with Mike, I was back in control, and I made my way to the bar to chat to some friends who had just arrived. They worked at the local hospital, and they reassured me that Derek would be fine because he had had an hour's rehearsal with all the flashing lights with no affect.

But, all during the show, my heart was in my mouth wondering if he was going to get through it all right. The only hiccup was that a fuse blew in one of the monitors and the electricity went off, but he stood for twenty minutes talking and keeping the audience's attention while the problem was rectified. A couple of times, he made a boob of introducing the wrong song but only minor things. I had also forgotten that some members of staff from Addenbrookes research unit were in the audience, so I'm sure they would have come to his aid if it had been needed.

One of the backing singers gave me a silk rose to give to Derek on stage. The other three had each got one, so I did not think anything about it. I also helped to arrange the songs in the show, but during the show everything stopped and Derek started to say how I had looked after him all during his recovery. Then, he called me out on stage to sit on a chair. I was still clutching the single silk rose when he presented me with a huge bouquet of flowers as a thank you. I smiled at Derek and then gave him the single rose, and he laughed and said, "Well, it's a fair exchange isn't it?" and then he performed our favourite Elvis song "The Wonder of You."

Derek was back on a high once again, really chuffed that money had been raised for the Air Ambulance and he had not lost the touch of his Elvis movements.

"I can still do it," he remarked once we were home.

Directly after a show it is impossible to go straight to bed and sleep, so we always sit enjoying a cup of tea or coffee and discuss the reactions of the audience that night. Sometimes, you get a lively crowd; another time, although enjoying the show, they are very quiet.

There seem to be three different categories of people that come to a show: firstly, those who genuinely support every show for whatever charity we are raising money for and at the same time are enjoying the show. It is very much appreciated by everyone concerned.

Secondly, there are those who only come to support a certain cause. Maybe we are raising money for a member of their family or a friend, and they never support anymore shows

Thirdly, there are the minority of desperate housewives, which I suppose they are having a midlife crisis, who think just because Elvis (Derek) gave them a scarf or sang a certain song to them, he'd only got eyes for them. This was when they started to invade our privacy.

After each concert, it would usually take Derek three or four days to come back to earth again, as the adrenalin put him on such a high. He would often telephone different members of the public, male and female, who were at the show, to find out their reactions. Did we do your favourite song? Did you like the supporting acts? What colour suit do you prefer? It was all harmless chat to see if there could be any improvements made for future shows, as we are always open to constructive criticism.

But two of these people were very devoted Elvis fans and began by texting uninteresting messages of how they had had their hair dyed, got new glasses, been shopping, sat having a cup of tea, a husband had trouble getting out of the end of the road on his way to work when it was icy, and so on. Why on earth they thought Derek would be interested in that information fails me, but over Christmastime 2011 it caused a laugh amongst friends and was a good after-dinner talking point.

Derek always said it was good public relations to chat to people and keep in with them and just to put bums on seats for any future shows, but later on, he changed his mobile number so only family and very close friends know it.

CHAPTER 48
Scotland

When, at last, in November 2007, Derek's car driving licence was granted it was a great relief. Derek had a little more independence after that and did not have to rely on me every time he wanted to go somewhere.

The funny thing was he never once suggested going for a ride with Gary in the truck, yet he had plenty of opportunities. I think it was because he was the one that was unable to drive.

Now his mood had changed for the better, he would open the back door and say, "I won't be long. I'm just popping out."

Christmas was fast approaching, and we were going to spend it in Scotland, just over the border in a cottage we had hired from friends. We would travel to Scotland by leaving in the early hours of the morning so we could reach the cottage during daylight hours, and if it was going to freeze that night, we would be able to make it along the track before it became too icy. The cottage was isolated and situated on the side of a hill. It was a couple of miles from the main road, and you had to get to it by a dirt track that gently climbed the closer you got to the cottage. If it was too icy, one had to rely on the nearby farmer to tow the car up to the cottage with his tractor.

Derek always loved driving, and never once did he suggest that I take over from him As he hadn't been driving since the

March, I left him to it. I did wonder how Derek would cope with the driving there, as it would take about seven hours, stopping once or twice to stretch our legs, but he was absolutely fine.

Although the cottage had electricity and running water, there was no television or central heating, only two storage heaters, one in the lounge and one in the hall. No telephone connected to the property, but that suited us down to the ground. We always carried our mobile phones with us anyway for emergencies.

If it was a cold, frosty morning, there would be ice on the inside of the windows in some of the rooms, but the bathroom was a different story. It felt like ice in there whatever time of day or night, when you sat on the toilet seat it was so cold one would always have to go "Aahhhhhh!" It reminded me of my childhood days before double glazing and central heating, unless you sat right in front of the fire and scorched, you always made sure you wore plenty of warm clothes.

We would go for long walks during the day, and then at night sit and read, play board games, cards, and also listen to the CDs we took with us, sitting next to a roaring coal fire with a nice glass of wine or spirits beside us. We knew we would have no visitors calling in on us during the dark nights.

The shepherd that worked on the farm would ride by the cottage during the day on his quad bike with two sheep dogs standing on the back of it. We stood watching at the window to see the dogs lean one way and then the other as the bike turned in different directions, but they always seemed to stay on the machine. On command, they would jump off and start to round the sheep up to take back to the farm buildings, for the forecast had talked of some winter weather coming.

Once the sheep were safely gathered in, the shepherd would make a point of stopping and coming in and having a Christmas drink with us before he made his way back home. He lived in a cottage with his wife at the entrance of the farm near the main road.

He would tell us of different experiences of being a shepherd and how years ago he had gotten caught up in a blizzard ("a white out" he called it) on the hills while checking the sheep and was completely lost until he came across a heap of stones, and then he knew exactly where he was. He really was a very dedicated shepherd.

We had been to the cottage before with friends, and we would say time did not matter once you arrived at the cottage. We always took the clock from the wall and hid it in a drawer, removed our wrist watches, and left them hidden in our luggage. I would tape an A4 chart on the back of the door with the date of each day we were spending at the cottage and beside each date write light and dark. Once daylight turned into dark, I would cross off daylight and then in the morning cross off dark so we always knew what day and date it was.

When we first started to take a break there, our friend who sometimes come with us, told his elderly mother what we did with the clock and watches once in the cottage.

She became very concerned and said, "Oh, but how do you know when to get up?"

Our friend replied, "When we wake up."

Then, she asked, "But how do you know when to eat?"

He replied, "When we're hungry."

"Well," she said, "you won't know what time to go to bed, will you?"

He replied, "Yes, when we are tired."

I don't really think she could come to terms with that idea at all.

Once we arrived back home after the holiday, Derek kept repeating, "I wonder how long before I can get my truck licence back?"

CHAPTER 49
Another Hospital Visit

When in November we had applied for Derek's car and truck licence, it was only his car licence that had been returned. The truck licence had been revoked, because the medical adviser at the Driving Vehicle Licensing Agency (DVLA) had recommended refusal due to the type of head injury Derek had suffered. He still could be prone to a seizure.

Two or three times a day, I would hear the same old story: "Wonder when I can have my truck licence back. Surely, I don't have to wait until September '08 before I can get an answer."

I told Derek he was lucky to be alive, let alone worrying about driving his dam truck again.

An appointment for March 12, 2008 came through the post to attend the research programme in the Wolfson Brain Imaging Centre for more computerized tests and another scan.

A few days later, another appointment arrived to attend the Traumatic Brain injury clinic a week after the tests and scans were taken to get the results of the tests. I then rang the secretary of the Traumatic Brain Injury clinic and asked if we could make an appointment for the same day as we lived a distance from the hospital and it was made for 3.00 p.m.

Then, Derek received another appointment to attend the Trauma Brain clinic again for October 2008 for the yearly follow-up. Derek was not prepared to wait until then. I said we could discuss this with the doctor on March 12.

Just as before, we sat in a small waiting room and were each given a questionnaire to fill in. This time, I could explain how Derek coped with performing the Elvis show.

Soon after, Derek was taken for his MRI scan. Once that was completed, we were taken to the same waiting area as before, where the next part of the tests was to take place. Again, we were given refreshments and had to wait about thirty minutes before a young lady came through to collect Derek. He had been very worried about doing this test, and I explained to the lady that Derek was never really very good at remembering things at the best of times. He was very good at doing mathematics in his head, whereas I would have to have a pen and paper to work it out, but then I had a good memory. This time, I was not allowed to go in with Derek while he did the computerized tests, as the lady said that sometimes the patient can be put off by knowing their partner was watching over them. I wished him luck as he walked off and the door closed behind him.

There I sat in the small waiting room. The television was on but with a very snowy picture, I could recognize the voices of a popular antiques programme, but could not see the items under the hammer. I was sitting on a settee opposite the television and kept getting up to adjust the aerial at the back of the set, but I could not improve the picture at all. Every channel was the same, so in the end I switched it off.

I sat reading a magazine but had no interest in it. I was just flicking through it, not really looking at the pages. I finally decided just to sit and wait for Derek to return.

Then, the door opened, and in he walked.

He blew out his cheeks and said, "I don't think I did very well this time."

Derek never did seem to have much confidence in himself. Whatever test he had taken in the past for his truck or tractor, he would always say, "I won't pass that," but he always did.

The lady researcher said that Derek had done very well. She said that the tests were identical to the previous ones, and they were to see if the brain had recovered anymore from the last time Derek was there.

Then, Derek would have to go along to the Trauma Brain Clinic to find out the results of the tests, as they were being emailed straight through to the clinic.

A few days prior to his appointment, I had suggested taking a DVD of the Elvis show to play on our small portable DVD player, so Derek could show the doctor how he had had no reaction from the lights and noise and how he had regained his strength enough to do all the Elvis moves. I had played the DVD and had stopped it on "Suspicious Minds", the fastest tempo song with the most moves in it.

When Derek was called in, as we walked through the door a man sitting at the desk introduced himself as one of the professors at the research centre, whom we knew by name but had not actually met before.

He said, "Ah, Elvis, come in" and shook both our hands. In the room sitting on the bed was one of the research team, who I had met on the ward, and two more students, one male and one female.

The professor asked some questions on how Derek had been doing, and then I explained how I had bought along a clip of the Elvis show and played the one track.

Once the song had finished, the professor said, "That's amazing. Would you mind if I kept the disc so I can show it to the students during my lectures, so they can see how a patient can recover so well from a traumatic head injury such as Derek had?"

Derek was only too pleased for him to keep it.

The professor looked at the notes in front of him and turned and looked at Derek and said, "Well, I'm sorry, but you can no longer help us in our research because you are too well now. I'm going to discharge you."

The Three Birds

Derek was very pleased and said, "Good, that's good. There is only one thing. I would like to apply for my truck licence, but the medical team at the DVLA has refused my application."

The professor looked at Derek and said, "I'm sorry but that is not in my department. You will have to talk to the doctor that was in charge of you."

We explained that his appointment was not until October. It was suggested we try to change it and make one earlier than October. I then asked if it would be possible to go to the NCCU to see if the nurse in charge was there so Derek could meet him.

The professor thought that was a brilliant idea as it is very rare that those nurses see the patient again once they have left that ward. We said our farewells and departed.

Once we were let in the critical-care unit, I was feeling nervous; I had been through that corridor so many times it was bringing it all back to me again.

The receptionist sat behind her desk and as I approached, she smiled and asked if she could help. Once I had explained why we were there, she lifted up the receiver and asked who could she say was waiting, and I laughed and said, "Say it's Elvis." Then speaking to someone, she put down the receiver and said he would be here in a minute.

A few minutes later the doors opened, and there was Nick. He was all smiles when he saw us, and he gave me a kiss and shook Derek's hand.

He said, "Oh, mate, it's so good to see you and looking so well. You're putting on weight."

We stood talking. Nick wanted to know what Derek had been doing.

Derek said to him, "So I was rough then when you last saw me?"

Nick replied, "You could say that." And then he held up his hand and putting his thumb and index finger almost together—I should think the gap between them was about one and an half to two mm—and said, "You were that close to not being here mate, but as you were an awkward old bugger and stubborn, you made it, along with the help of your wife here."

Just as we stood talking, the door from the ward opened, and the doctor that was usually on duty on the NCC ward walked through. He immediately turned right along a short corridor, where I had seen the white coats hanging on pegs. At the end of the corridor was a door where only staff where allowed. Shortly afterwards, the doctor came back out wearing casual clothes with a rucksack hanging from his shoulder, and he walked by us.

I said, "Derek, that was one of the doctors who looked after you."

Then, Nick called him back and introduced him to Derek. The doctor stood there with tears in his eyes, unable to speak. The doctor then commented to Nick on how they never got to see the patients and the end result once they had left hospital. He just said, "Unbelievable", shook Derek's hand again, and then left.

After a few more minutes talking, Nick excused himself as he had to get back on duty. He shook hands and left and we made our way back to the car.

Derek was pleased he had met the doctors and staff that had helped to look after him while in hospital, but the same question rose again, could I change the appointment to see the doctor so he could get his truck licence back. With a sigh, I said I would ring the next day.

CHAPTER 50

Truck Licence

The very next morning, I rang to make another appointment for Derek with the doctor at Addenbrookes to see if he could get his truck licence back again. After several attempts, I finally got through to the trauma clinic and made an appointment for April 21, 2008.

It would not be so long for Derek to wait. We carried on the daily routines until the day finally arrived to travel back to the hospital.

Again, we sat in this overcrowded waiting room waiting for Derek's turn. Almost forty five minutes later, the nurse called Derek in. We both sat in front of the consultant who was sitting reading the notes that were on the desk in front of him. He looked up, and Derek explained why we had come to the hospital now instead of waiting until October.

The consultant asked a few questions and then said there is no way you can get your truck licence back for at least three, five, or ten years, but I doubt if it will be ten. Derek tried to argue, and the consultant said he would contact the Driving Vehicle Licensing Agency. We were dismissed from the room.

All the way home, it was murder just to sit and listen to Derek go on and on about his licence, but once we got home I said, "Well, you do something about it. I have filled in forms, changed appointments, and done everything I know of. Now, you can do it."

The next morning Derek rang the ministry and asked their opinion of the situation and was told to appeal against the decision. So it was onto the internet to print off yet another set of forms, and there I was filling them in. Once they were posted, we had to sit and wait for a reply.

After weeks of waiting for a reply, which never came, I then suggested to Derek to ring the DVLA to ask if they had any information regarding the forms that we had sent to them or any news from the consultant at Addenbrookes.

The DVLA told Derek that they did not know why he had appealed, as they had not heard from the hospital and suggested ringing the hospital to get them to send details to the DVLA. On finally contacting the hospital, we were told that they no longer notified the DVLA unless it was requested. Once again, we rang back the DVLA and explained the situation. They said they did not contact the hospitals any more, so it turned out to be a stalemate.

We had made numerous telephone calls, written letters, sent emails to and fro, and it was now getting beyond a joke, so I turned to Derek and said to him, "Go private. Other people pay and go for a private consultation, so why can't you?"

Derek then rang the local private hospital and left a message on their answer phone. The secretary rang back in the late afternoon and explained that Derek would have to make an appointment with his GP. Then, once his GP had contacted that department, an appointment would come through the post.

So, then we made a visit to the local surgery and a letter was sent to the private hospital. Days after, an appointment came through the post for July 9, 2008.

The day soon arrived, and it was off to the hospital. I always made sure I was available to attend the appointments in order to make sure Derek understood all the information given to him. The neurology consultant was a very pleasant man. After asking many questions in great detail, many of which I had to answer as Derek could not remember them because they were about the days following Derek's recovering from the coma. After the questions, the consultant took Derek through to an adjoining room for a further examination.

As we left, the consultant said we would be receiving a letter from him in due course.

Patiently waiting for that letter to arrive, every morning Derek went to the letterbox and said, "Nothing from the hospital today."

Then it arrived. As Derek tore open the envelope he passed the letter to me and repeated, "Read it, read it," as I could read faster than he could.

The letter went on to explain the initial injuries of the accident and how we had applied for the license and been refused because of the risk of a seizure. The bottom paragraph read:

> Based on figures in a 1998 publication of a journal of medicine, patients like you who have had a severe head injury, have a 5.8 per cent risk of having a seizure in the first year after the injury and then a 0.9 per cent risk per year in years two to five. Most of this risk will be in the early parts of these periods, and so I would estimate that the current risk would probably be around the 2 per cent mark.

The consultant requested that the DVLA look at this LGV application again and would be happy to write a report direct to the DVLA if they contacted him.

Derek's face said it all. I sat down straight away at the computer and wrote a letter direct to the medical board at the DVLA and enclosed a copy of the letter from the consultant and posted it at once.

When I arrived back from posting the letter I told Derek not to get his hopes up to high as the DVLA medical team might not approve it straight away.

It was a waiting game once more, and at the end of November 2008, finally the letter came that we had been waiting for: Yes, Derek had been approved. He had recovered enough for him to have his truck licence back.

He was then on his mobile ringing his mechanic to see when he was available to come and overhaul his beloved truck and get it ready for the road once more. It had to have a Ministry of Transport test, so it had to be in good order. It had been standing in the shed since March 2007, and things would have seized up or perished, so there would be plenty of replacement work to do on it.

In January 2009, the big red and white truck and trailer left the yard with a confident and delighted driver. I, for one, never expected I would see the day that Derek would ever drive that vehicle again, not because I had no trust in him, but because how bad his injuries were two years previous.

CHAPTER 51

Helicopter Trip and a Buckingham Palace Visit

It has not been all doom and gloom.

On Derek's sixtieth birthday, I surprised him by organizing a birthday party at a village hall, not only to celebrate his birthday but his life as well, as I never thought he would survive to see it.

As a present, Stuart, Caroline, and their children, presented Derek with a voucher for two for a helicopter trip from Norwich airport.

Stuart said, "There you are Dad—a trip in a helicopter for you and Mum, but this time you will be awake to enjoy it."

We waited a few weeks before booking the trip, and Stuart and Caroline came along to watch. On arriving at the airport we were shown into a waiting area in a small room. Sitting in the room was about ten other people, but only two would fly in the helicopter with us, the rest were family or friends come along to take photographs. We were told that the pilot would soon be there to give a briefing before lift off. The door opened and in walked the doctor who had attended Derek at the scene of his accident and also travelled in the Air Ambulance to Addenbrookes. He was also surprised to see Derek sitting there.

He told us he was also a trained pilot and flew the helicopter pleasure trips in his spare time.

The pilot came over and shook Derek's hand. Then he turned to the other people in the room and introduced Derek to them. He gave them a short account of his accident and then said, "This is the luckiest man alive."

Once we were given some health and safety instructions, Derek, I, and two other people made our way to the helicopter. It was a tossup who sat in the front with the pilot. A teenager, the youngest of the four, sat in the front, and we climbed in the back.

It was a glorious day. Chilly, but the sun shining made it rather warm inside the helicopter. Rather than fly over the city, the pilot headed toward the Norfolk Broads and gave out information on various points of interest below us. The twenty-minute flight was soon over but was very enjoyable.

One morning, the telephone rang and a voice asked to speak to Derek Russell.

I replied, "He would not be home until later that day."

The lady said who she was and asked if we had ever attended the Queen's Garden Party at Buckingham Palace.

I said, "No."

She then gave three dates. I had to choose one to attend, and if we were accepted we would receive an invitation.

On June 6, the cream-coloured envelope arrived with the official stamp of "ER" with the crown sitting on the top of the letters, with another oval-shape stamp at the bottom with "Lord Chamberlain" at the top, the crown in the centre, and then Buckingham Palace at the bottom of it.

I waited with baited breath until Derek arrived home and saw the look on his face when I handed him the envelope.

He opened it up and took out a very thick, white card invitation with the embossed crown and letters "ER" in gold. It read as follows:

THE LORD CHAMBERLAIN IS
Commanded by Her Majesty to invite

Mr and Mrs Derek Russell

To a Garden Party
At Buckingham Palace
On Tuesday 14 July 2009 from 4 to 6 p.m.

We both assumed we had been invited because of the charity work we had done and would be representing all the Elvis team. Also in the envelope was an information leaflet of the do's and don'ts of the day and a car-parking ticket number if arriving by car.

The big day arrived, and our son Stuart and daughter-in-law Caroline travelled with us on the train to London. Once we were inside Buckingham Palace, they would go off sightseeing and meet us back outside the gates later.

There were two or three professional photographers standing near the railings of the Palace and doing a roaring trade taking individual photographs, and I must admit we had our photograph taken by one.

We were the fifth couple in the queue outside the centre gates. It was lovely to stand and watch all the ladies' fashion and visitors from all over the world, who were sightseeing and taking photographs of the queues standing there. We queued for about an hour, and then the police opened the gates and we were led across the front courtyard, through the arch way underneath the famous balcony, across another courtyard, up some steps, and through the doors of Buckingham Palace. We handed our printed cards (not the white invitation which we were able to keep) to a security guard. Walking on the deep red carpet, on our left, passing the stairs that seemed to go on forever, also covered in the red carpet with family portraits hanging on the wall along the staircase, we were then ushered through some French doors to the outside of the Palace. We went down several stone steps and walked onto to the lawn. To our left were several tables and chairs lined up, and not one out of place. Behind them was an open-fronted marquee where the buffet was laid. Standing to attention at each pillar of the marquee were servants dressed in black trousers, cream shirts, and a black bow tie, their hands covered with white gloves. We went and sat down. Then, a mother and daughter joined us at the table, as the chairs became quickly filled. Over the opposite side of the lawn was a large gazebo where the military band sat playing in red and black uniform. Another marquee was standing next to the bandstand and this was where the royal party were to sit to have their afternoon tea.

It was amazing just to sit and watch the sea of guests' heads coming down the steps onto the lawn. There was every nationality, some with the most colourful and traditional outfits of their country. We were told that eight-thousand guests attended that day and the same for the other two garden parties as well.

As the royal party made their entrance and stood at the top of the stone steps, the band began playing the national anthem. Seated guests stood up to join in the singing. Then, as the Queen and other royal members made their way down the steps, there were a small number of individual presentations that had been pre-arranged to meet the Queen. Then, gentlemen in arms formed a lane for the royal party to move through the guests. There were so many people now standing between us and the royals it was impossible to even get a glimpse of them.

We made our way over to the buffet area, where we were each given a small tray to place your sandwiches and cakes at one end, and at the other end was a small circular indentation where you could place your cup or glass. We were then directed into different queues of guests ready to choose our finger sandwiches and really lovely dainty fruit tarts and cakes. We could either have tea, coffee, orange juice, or water. Then, we made our way back to the table, so the mother and daughter who had been on guard keeping our seats made their way to the buffet area. We all sat talking and admiring the different dress creations. Once finished eating, Derek said he would like to go for a walk along the lake at the bottom end of the lawn, so we said our farewells and left the table.

As we walked along the lawn the crowd had started to disburse and we stood only feet away from the royal party as they were being introduced to members of the public.

I saw the sign for the toilets, and said I must have a royal flush. Luckily, there were only about five people in the queue, so I did not have to wait long. As I came back and found Derek, everyone around seemed to be eating an ice cream. I asked one lady where she had acquired hers from, and she said that young lads were walking round giving them out. As we reached the lake, a young man approached us with a large tray containing small tubs of ice creams and offered us one each. We then strolled round the lake, stopping to look back at the palace in the background. The only photograph we have is in our memory, as we were not allowed to take a camera with us on the day. We made our way to the flower beds that were dotted about. The weather could not have been better—it was a lovely, sunny afternoon with a light wind blowing, not to hot.

All too soon, it was time to leave. We headed for the side gate where we had arranged to meet my cousin and his partner for a drink in the local along the road. Several people were walking along the pavement dressed in their finery, so everyone knew where they had been. We met my cousin and his partner and went into the pub for a drink and catch-up on the day's events. Then, after letting Stuart know where he would find us, we made our way back to the underground to Victoria Station and then the journey home. It was an experience not likely to ever happen again.

CHAPTER 52
Four and Half Years Later, 2011

It has been a long road to recovery for Derek. There have been several little incidents, far too many to mention, but one I can recall, was when the grandsons made ramps outside in the yard so they could ride their bikes over them.

Derek walked by and said straight away, "I hope you're going to clear all that wood up," and he came in the house and moaned about the mess they were making.

Six months later, he was encouraging them to make the ramps and saying it will do them more good playing outside than sitting in front of a computer screen, which before his accident he would have encouraged them.

He has been short tempered and done things way out of character for him, but I must stress that Derek had never acted or been violent at any time.

He has also made comments to people that have made me cringe, but when confronting him about it, he said he had not realized he had said anything wrong. So, if Derek has been outspoken to you, then I can only say he did not mean to upset you.

During the autumn months of 2010, Derek seemed extra agitated and stressed; I kept asking him if he was OK. He would always answer very abruptly, "Yes, why?" I knew something was wrong but did not know what.

At bedtime, we always read before we went to sleep, but just lately he would always get into bed, turn his back on me, lie down and go straight to sleep. I would often say, "Give us a cuddle," and he would reply, "In a minute," and the next thing he was snoring his head off. He never showed me any affection at all. Thoughts crept into my head: *Was he seeing someone else?* Although he was at work all day and we only ever went out together, at times I felt really stressed.

On New Year's Eve, we always have family and close friends round to the house to celebrate the New Year.

It was just after midnight when he came to me and said out of the blue, "Oh well, we're now in the year of our fortieth wedding anniversary," and walked off.

The last of the friends left around 2.15 a.m., and it was off to bed.

I commented on why he had said this. He just replied, "Well it is."

The next day, we were busy clearing up after the night before: rearranging furniture and putting glasses and dishes away that only get used for special occasions. After we had eaten, we took the dogs for a walk. Once back home and having made a hot drink, we sat down to relax for the evening. Derek sat on the settee looking really miserable.

All of a sudden he said, "What would you say if I did not go to work anymore?"

I replied, "That's up to you."

He still looked glum, and I said, "For god's sake cheer up. Things could be worse."

He replied, "Like what?"

I answered, "You could be an invalid in a wheelchair or have cancer."

I was totally shocked when he said, "I think I have."

"What do you mean?" I asked, almost in tears.

He said, "I noticed a lump in one of my testicles about six months ago, and it's growing larger."

"Why on earth did you not say anything to me?" I asked.

He uttered, "I just couldn't, because I knew you would make me go to the doctors. That would mean hospital, then an operation, then that's it. After you're opened up, the cancer spreads quickly, so I'd rather just let it takes its course. You have had enough to go through, without me adding to it once again. I'm really not afraid of dying; it's what you would have to face leading up to it."

I took him in my arms and said, "Oh, Derek, I'm making you an appointment to see the GP on Tuesday morning, whether you like it or not."

It was only Saturday, and the surgery was not open anymore until Tuesday morning due to the New Year holidays. It was going to be long weekend.

We could not eat or sleep properly. As soon as I stepped out of bed, I was retching until mid-morning. We sat talking to each other.

Derek said, "I just hope I can make just one more holiday in May. I doubt I will be able to take Gaby (our only granddaughter) to her prom evening in July. No more concerts. Maybe I won't see another Christmas."

I just took him in my arms and said, "We'll get through this together; I'll be here for you as always."

Tuesday morning could not come soon enough. As soon as the surgery was open, I rang for an appointment for that morning, as the surgery closes at lunchtime on Tuesdays, only to be told it was for emergencies only. I asked if our GP could ring me back. About ten minutes later, our doctor rang back, and I explained the situation and was told to go to the surgery at 10.30 a.m., so he could see what was going on.

As we were about to walk out the door, Derek said, "You'll be sorry. This is the beginning of the end."

Neither of us spoke as we made our ten-minute journey there. I could not believe it when we drove on the car park: my brother's car was in the car park.

As we neared the doors to go in the waiting room, Derek murmured, "The beginning of the end."

There sat my brother, and we took seats near him. He explained he was there to see the nurse, and I just said Derek had a nasty boil and thought the doctor should see it. My brother was called in the nurse's room, and soon after it was Derek's turn.

We walked into the doctor's room, and straight away he ushered Derek into an adjoining examination room and closed the door. Minutes later, the door opened and the doctor came through.

I heard Derek say, "Will you tell this lady here?"

Shaking his head from side to side, the doctor said, "No, definitely not cancer."

A smiling Derek walked through the door and said, "Thank God."

The doctor explained that sometimes a small tear appears in the wall of the testicle and fluid seeps through and feels like a lump and that it could be easily repaired.

We walked back to the car, and once inside, we both sat with tears running down our cheeks.

Derek took hold of my hand and said, "Thank you for making me see the doctor."

I replied, "Derek, if only you had told me before, it would have saved all the stress both of us have gone through over these last few months."

Once home, Derek took out his wallet, opened it, and removed the plastic bag that contained the cloth necklace, "The Green Scapular," that Sue's friend had given him in Addenbrookes. He looked at it and said, "Thank you. That's the second time you have given me my life back."

Derek still carries it in his wallet with him at all times.

So, guys, if you notice a change in your genitals, please, please, go and see your doctor immediately and get it checked out. It will save a lot of stress on relationships and ease your own mind.

I thought—or assumed, I should say—that Derek was back to normal health again, but in body, not mind, which has taken much longer to heal. It's been very hard for me at times to understand some of the stages Derek has gone through.

As just an examples, was how at one time he kept going on about wood—yes, wood. We have a supply of off-cut wood to heat our two wood-burning systems. Whenever our son Stuart was with his dad, the only conversation they ever had was about wood: collecting it, moving it, cutting it, stacking it, and burning it. In end, whenever Stuart knew his dad was outside, he avoided going out there.

Stuart said, "I would like nothing more than to be outside with Dad talking about the weather, motor racing, aircraft, Elvis concerts—anything but *wood*."

In the end, I had to tell Derek to talk to Stuart about something else. Even sitting in the house at night he would keep on about the wood to me, but it gradually got better.

Another obsession was his need to have two mobiles. If he dropped one and damaged it, he would have to replace it with another cheap one. He called me sometimes from a different number, and I would query it with him when he got home. He said he had to use one of the men's phones he was working with. A couple of weeks later, I was cleaning his car out that he uses for work, as he had borrowed a tractor from work over the weekend and had driven it back to the farm that morning, as Derek and Gary sold their trucks and each independently working for different employers, Derek chose to work on an arable farm, leaving the car at home in a filthy state inside. On the front seat was a mobile phone booklet with a mobile number scribbled on the front.

After thinking about it for a while, I decided to call the number. I had used an old mobile I had gotten, as he would have forgotten that number. It began to ring, and then he answered it. I said he had better start explaining what was going on. He burst into tears and said he would ring me back. I waited and waited. After twenty minutes, I called him back, and he was still crying. We chatted, and I called him at least ten times throughout the day, as he seemed so distraught. I told him we would talk when he got home.

After we had discussed the problem at some length, later on that night Derek came to me and started to cry.

"Please help me," he sobbed. He said he did not know why he had the desperation for another phone when he already had a perfectly good mobile. "How can I forget about it when adverts are forever coming on the television and people all around me are going on about their mobiles all the time?"

I said I would help him as much as possible to overcome this problem.

(Can you remember reading about his mobile phone antics earlier in the book?)

On seeking professional medical advice, I was told it all stemmed from the head injury, which could be helped by counselling, but Derek refused to seek any stranger's advice. As a result, we have helped each other through this, and his sheer determination has won the battle.

He said, "I gave up smoking about twenty odd years ago without counselling, so why not get through this without counselling?"

And we have.

I made Derek promise me that if the need for another mobile overpowered him, he was to call me and we would chat to take his mind off it. The following four or five days would be crucial, as I only ever usually called him at work during his lunch breaks. He didn't call me unless it was to tell me he was going to be home later than usual, but I'm afraid the first couple of days we called each other several times during the day, as I could hear Derek was stressed and was very concerned. On the third day, he called me when he arrived at work and then three times more during the day, but seemed less stressed.

I had already told Derek I had a spare mobile if he ever had the urge to take it with him, if he felt safe knowing he had a spare one. During his break time, Derek called me, and if he seemed unusually quiet, I would talk him round.

On the fourth day, he called me and openly admitted he was trying to think how he could convince me that his original mobile was not working properly so he could take mine.

Then, he said, "I thought, *Snap out of it you bloody fool.*"

Nothing much was mentioned until about three weeks after. He began to openly mention that his addiction for another mobile phone was so strong and that he could not understand why it was so important to him. We began to laugh about it. Now, four months later, he says he never thinks about it, and he thanked me for helping him through another rough patch of his life.

SO WELL DONE

The strangest thing happened today. A complete stranger came to the door delivering leaflets. I saw the figure through the frosted glass and opened the door. He was looking for the letter box, which I explained was fixed to the gate. He then asked if I was related to Derek, as he knew he had a truck and drag. This man said he had also driven one years ago. I explained to him about Derek's accident and said that due to the economic climate both trucks had been sold and father and son were now working for different companies. He then went on to tell me that he also had had head and hand injuries caused by an incident with a truck. He told his story, and there were so many similarities relating to the same problems that Derek had suffered. By this time, Derek had arrived home, and he came to join in on the conversation. Another story this guy told was that he used to talk to himself; he would hold a complete conversation and would answer himself as well, just as though there were two people there. At this, I was so over whelmed, I just started to cry.

Derek made another surprising remark: "That the first time I was allowed home from the hospital for a short while, I felt so safe and secure when I was lying on the settee, with the dog Barney by my side and the sound of the clock ticking. No one could see me and come to get me. They would have to get past you first and then the dog, and I knew you would not let anyone come in and get me."

At once, I realized why he had kept hiding up behind his truck when he heard footsteps or cars on the gravel. He must have felt more secure hiding, so no one would take him back to hospital. "Out of sight, out of mind."

I have often thought at times, *How on earth have I managed to cope with these situations?* But when you love someone as much as I love Derek, you seem to have an inner strength that helps you get through it.

EPILOGUE

It is now the end of December 2011. From the first time I read this book to Derek in July of this year, he has certainly been a changed man. Whatever was bottled up inside him was released on that night, after hearing the first chapter. The stress has disappeared, and he is back to the loving husband and family man he was before the accident.

I emailed the professor at Addenbrookes to ask why, after all this time, Derek was suddenly interested in his accident after hearing the book; I told him how much it had changed our lives for the better.

The professor replied and explained that often patients who sustain a traumatic brain injury find that they have lost a chunk of memory covering the period of acute illness. This loss is a lot more complete than the period of unawareness that we experience when we are asleep. This may be because the injury reduces function of even background brain activity that persists when we are asleep. While reasons for this are unclear, they have found that patients benefit from understanding the narrative of their illness, even though they can sometimes be distressed when they first hear about it.

If you ever find yourself in this situation, never give up; have faith and try to stay positive, but it's something you cannot get through without the help and support of family and true friends. I stress the word *friends* carefully, as some whom you think of as friends can turn round and stab you in the back.

It has been a long roller-coaster ride, a journey that could have ended in disaster.

We as a family have been very fortunate that Derek has come full circle; he is able to do all the things he's always loved doing, and he does not have to take any medication for the traumatic head injury he suffered.

The only thing is that Derek has lost his sense of smell. He says he misses the smells of fresh-baked bread, opening a new jar of coffee, cakes I have baked coming out of a hot oven, or the wisteria in bloom on the front of the house, but he has not lost his taste and says that's just as important to him.

Your confidence, willpower, and determination will brush off onto your loved one and help him or her to recover, however long it takes.

As Derek said, "It must have helped me; otherwise, why am I still here?"

The most important thing is to always be there for each other.

After many hours of talking, crying, and laughing, we have just raised our full glasses to toast each other in the future:

To love, health, and happiness for the rest of our lives together.

CHE SARÀ, SARÀ

A MESSAGE FROM DEREK

In July 2011, on completion of this book, my wife, Christine, started to read it out to me. After the first two chapters, we were locked in each other's arms, sobbing. Chris, as I call her, knew she would break down as she said, "She always did when trying to write about it, let alone read it out."

I myself did not have a clue what to expect, and without warning it really did knock the stuffing out of me. I cannot believe the man in this story is actually me.

Upon listening to this story for the first time, although I was vaguely aware of what had happened to me, I now fully understand all the hard work and effort many dedicated people put in to help with my recovery.

First of all I would like to thank the doctors, the nurses, and all the other medical staff at Addenbrookes NCCU for all their hard work and dedication. I thank also the research team involved in my care, as the research they did ten years ago went a long way to help me now. I feel so privileged that I was taken to the world's leading neurology hospital. As I understand it, patients suffering with neurology problems come from all over the world to Addenbrookes hospital, as well as students to listen to the professor give his lectures. Also, my gratitude goes to the Queen Elizabeth Hospital, King's Lynn, for looking after me on the short-term stay upon my transfer.

At this stage, I would like to stress that so many people complain about the NHS treatment, but I could not have had been cared for any better or quicker, even if I had been a private patient.

More of my thanks goes to the two men at the factory who attended me at the scene while waiting for medical assistance to arrive, and the local ambulance service and the East Anglian Air Ambulance team for their speed and expertise to administer drugs at the scene and en route to Cambridge.

I did not realize all the effort that was made by family and friends, by just being there to offer Chris help whatever or whenever she needed it, especially our sons, Gary and Stuart, along with their wives, Anna and Caroline.

Without this kind of assistance it would have been much harder for her to be by my bedside as many hours as she was, which I'm sure made a vital difference.

I very much appreciated all the cards, gifts, and good wishes that I received from everyone, including friends in Western Canada.

This has been a very emotional journey, which has been emphasized by listening to Chris reading this story out to me, especially when I heard the story about the female blackbird, which is the only strong memory I have of my stay at Addenbrookes.

I would also like to say, this is the first time I have totally understood the trauma of the past four and half years that my wife has been put through. As I now realize, I have acted like a right pain in the a-e to her, which I would like us both to put behind us so that we can concentrate on our future together. ("I was blind, but now can see; was lost, but now am found".) To me it just proves the dedication, love, and respect she still has for me after forty years of marriage, as I have for her, even more so now, if that could ever be possible.

THIS IS THE REASON I AM STILL ALIVE

For me to say thank you seems so inadequate for the way I feel about all the people who have been named in this book, along with many more, too many to mention. But I know there were not any who gave their time, effort, and wishes just for publicity purposes. They gave it freely for me and Chris from the bottom of their hearts.

At the beginning of December, a complete stranger to Chris rang for some tickets for our concert (I knew him, as when working outside his house he would call me in for a cup of coffee). He said he knew Derek and all about his accident. Chris remarked how much better I had been since hearing the story she had written, and he remarked that all the demons had gone then. Yes, I now think they have.

I would like to dedicate these words of this song "The Wonder of You" to one and all.

> When no one else can understand me
> When everything I do is wrong
> You give me hope and consolation
> You give me strength to carry on

I was then given the opportunity to name this book. It did not take me too long to think about it:

THREE BIRDS THAT SAVED MY LIFE

First was the big yellow bird (East Anglian Air Ambulance), which the pilot described as the fastest bird.

Second was the blackbird in Addenbrookes garden that shocked my memory back, as it came closer to me than nature would normally allow.

Third was my wife, Chris, who was always there and helped me overcome many problems that I have suffered.

All I can say to one and all for helping to give me my life back is, with my greatest gratitude,

THANK YOU.